Don't Get Killed on Taxes

Praise for *Don't Get Killed on Taxes*

In *Don't Get Killed On Taxes*, P. J. DiNuzzo and Steven Jarvis use clear, everyday language to debunk myths and explain strategies and tools available for thoughtful tax planning. Drawing on their decades of experience, P.J. and Steven focus on the long term, helping identify ways that advisors can navigate the complex subject of taxes while still providing personalized financial advice and customized solutions for investors. The result is a book that will appeal to advisors and investors alike.

—**Dave Butler,** Chief Executive Officer,
Dimensional Fund Advisors

Private Wealth Advisor, P. J. DiNuzzo has helped hundreds of families navigate the ever-changing world of tax planning. In *Don't Get Killed on Taxes*, P. J. and Steven Jarvis are now giving you the tools and ideas that can help you ensure you pay exactly what you owe in taxes every year, and nothing more.

—**Dr. Glenn Vo,** *Wall Street Journal* and *USA Today*
bestselling author of *Industry Influencer*

Don't Get Killed on Taxes guides you step by step on how to navigate your taxes. No matter your unique situation, P. J. DiNuzzo and Steven Jarvis will help you dispel the myths, minimize your taxable income, and never fear Tax Day again.

—**Chris Tuff,** *USA Today* best selling author of
The Millennial Whisperer and *Save Your Asks*

Don't Get Killed on Taxes is the complete handbook for not only tax savings but also offers practical steps to grow and protect your financial legacy. This book should be read by everyone who is serious about strategically saving on their taxes and building a strong financial future! –

—**NJ Rongner,** co-founder, Helm Advisory Group

Don't Get Killed on Taxes is THE handbook for understanding how to minimize your tax liability without the stress or confusion that typically comes with taxes. This book is definitely a go-to for me when mapping out my clients' tax strategies to keep more of their money in their pockets.

—**Dr. Portia R. Jackson,** CFP®, Wealth Coach for Entrepreneurs

DON'T GET KILLED ON TAXES

20 of the Most Common Reasons You're Sending Too Much Money to the IRS

From *Wall Street Journal* & *USA Today* Best-Selling Author

P.J. DiNuzzo, CPA, PFS™, MBA, MSTx
and Steven Jarvis, CPA, MBA

NEW YORK

LONDON • NASHVILLE • MELBOURNE • VANCOUVER

Don't Get Killed on Taxes

20 of the Most Common Reasons You're Sending Too Much Money to the IRS

Published in New York, New York, by Morgan James Publishing. Morgan James is a trademark of Morgan James, LLC. www.MorganJamesPublishing.com

Proudly distributed by Ingram Publisher Services.

Morgan James BOGO™

A **FREE** ebook edition is available for you or a friend with the purchase of this print book.

CLEARLY SIGN YOUR NAME ABOVE

Instructions to claim your free ebook edition:
1. Visit MorganJamesBOGO.com
2. Sign your name CLEARLY in the space above
3. Complete the form and submit a photo of this entire page
4. You or your friend can download the ebook to your preferred device

ISBN 9781636980423 paperback
ISBN 9781636980430 ebook
Library of Congress Control Number: 2022944891

Cover & Interior Design by:
Christopher Kirk
www.GFSstudio.com

Morgan James is a proud partner of Habitat for Humanity Peninsula and Greater Williamsburg. Partners in building since 2006.

Get involved today! Visit MorganJamesPublishing.com/giving-back

IMPORTANT DISCLOSURE INFORMATION

Patrick J. DiNuzzo, CPA, PFS™, AIF®, MBA, MSTx, is the founder and Chief Executive Officer of DiNuzzo Private Wealth ("DPW"), an investment adviser registered with the United States Securities and Exchange Commission, located in Beaver, PA, and Pittsburgh.

Steven Jarvis, CPA, MBA, is the co-founder, CEO and Head CPA of Retirement Tax Services ("RTS"), a tax firm serving clients across the country through tax preparation and tax planning.

The book content is for information purposes only and does not provide any personalized advice from the author to the reader that is based upon the reader's specific situation or objectives. To the contrary, no reader should assume that this book serves as the receipt of, or a substitute for, personalized advice from the investment and/or tax professionals of his/her choosing. Please remember that different types of investments involve varying degrees of risk. Therefore, it should not be assumed that future performance of any specific investment, or investment or tax strategy (including the investments and/or investment and tax strategies referenced and/or recommended in the book), or any noninvestment related content (including financial planning issues), will be profitable, equal any historical performance levels, be suitable for a reader's individual situation, or prove correct. Certain portions of the book may reflect positions and/or recommendations as of a specific prior date, and may no longer be reflective of current positions, recommendations, or laws. **Please Note: Limitations**. Neither rankings and/or recognitions by unaffiliated rating services, publications, media, or other organizations, nor the achievement of any professional designation, certification, degree, or license, membership in any professional organization, or any amount of prior experience or success, should be construed by a client or prospective client as a guarantee that he/she will experience a certain level of results if DPW and RTS is engaged, or continues to be engaged, to provide services. Rankings published by magazines, and others, generally base their selections exclusively on information prepared and/or submitted by the recognized adviser. Rankings are generally limited to participating advisers (participation criteria/methodology available at www.dinuzzo.com). No ranking or recognition should be construed as a current or past endorsement of DPW or RTS by any of their clients. A copy of DPW's current written disclosure brochure discussing its services and fees continues to be available at www.dinuzzo.com.

Additionally, names and identifying details have been changed to protect the privacy of the individuals whose stories have been used in the book to demonstrate the principles discussed. Any resemblance of the people referenced to actual persons, living or dead, or actual events is purely coincidental.

Dedication from P. J.

This Book Is Dedicated to:
Pasquale (Patsy) and Rose
Joe and Anna
Natale (Ned) and Phyllis
Nick and Renee
Mike, Jessica, and Estelle
Patsy, Michaela, Lucca, and Pasquale
Renee, Avery, and Danica
Mark and Jackie
Ashley and Sam
Thank you for your faith, family, hard work, loyalty, authenticity, genuineness, gratitude, appreciation, heritage, tradition, legacy, guidance, wisdom, time, patience, passion, understanding, support, and listening.
If you weren't you, I could never be me.
I love all of you and am forever IN Gratitude™ for the immeasurable gifts you have provided me during my life.

Dedication from Steven

This book is dedicated to:
Kelsey

You have always believed I am capable of great things and somehow have had the patience and dedication to support me throughout this journey. Nothing I have accomplished would be a reality without you.

Evelyn and Caden

I haven't always made it easy, but I couldn't ask for better people to be on my team. We do hard things—Team Honey Badger for life.

Table of Contents

Special Recognition and Gratitude

It takes a village to be able to produce a book like
Don't Get Killed on Taxes.
I thank many of those people in the acknowledgments section
of this book.
However, two people's contributions were so important and pivotal to
both this book and my ability to provide my clients with the tax plan-
ning and strategy they need to minimize their tax liabilities and maxi-
mize their control over their future.
As such, I'd like to take this moment to recognize Jennifer B. Reddinger,
Management Team, VP, EA, CFP®, AIF®, Tax and Wealth Advisor; and
Kenneth M. McDaniel, EA, AIF®, Tax Advisor—two key members of
my advisory team, who worked tirelessly (through tax season!) to ensure
Don't Get Killed on Taxes includes the most important strategies that we
use at DiNuzzo Wealth Management to make a real impact
on our clients' lives.
Without them, this book would not be nearly as helpful as it is.
Thank you both.
P. J.

Acknowledgments from P. J.

D on't *Get Killed on Taxes* could not have been written without the contributions and input over my lifetime of many family members, team members, individuals, organizations, and the Dimensional Fund Advisors (DFA) team and research department.

Special thanks to my advisory team and their areas of expertise: Mark S. DiNuzzo, Executive Committee Member, Executive VP, CFP˚, AIF˚, MBA, Retirement Planning/Risk Management, Wealth Advisor; Michael V. DiNuzzo, Executive Committee Member, Senior VP, CFP˚, ChFC˚, MSFS, AIF˚, Retirement Planning/Risk Management, Wealth Advisor; Carl J. Hartman, Senior VP, Senior Investment Officer, ChFC˚, AIF˚, Retirement Planning/Investment Management, Wealth Advisor; Jacob R. Potts, Management Team Leader, VP, CFP˚, ChFC˚, AIF˚, Portfolio Management Trade Team Leader, Wealth Advisor; Robert F. Graham, VP, AIF˚, MBA, VP Retirement Planning, Wealth Advisor; Leslie D. Taylor-Neumann, Management Team, VP, Wealth Planning Team Leader, AIF˚, Wealth Advisor; Jennifer B. Reddinger, Management Team, VP, EA, CFP˚, AIF˚, Tax and Wealth Advisor; and Kenneth M. McDaniel, EA, AIF˚, Tax Advisor.

Additional special thanks to my fellow team members in our operations department: Jackie DiNuzzo, Executive Committee Member,

Compliance Officer/Office Manager; Lisa Faulkner, Senior Client Service Specialist; Terri Tepsic, Property Manager; Mikey Ronacher, Client Performance Team Leader; Brooke McMaster, Management Team, Senior Client Service Specialist; Cliff Smith, IT Director; Ken Aikens, Client Service Specialist; Jeff Buckley, Client Service Specialist; Michael Cindrich, Director of First Impressions/Tax Team; Suzanne Boren, Executive Assistant, Culture and HR Team Leader; Renee Foody, Administrative Assistant; Denise Lyons, Bookkeeping Manager; Nick DiNuzzo, Video/Internet Manager; Rose Dessler, Compliance Officer/HR Manager; and the Matriarch of our family, Phyllis Nutz (DiNuzzo), Client Service (Emeritus).

Attorneys: Ed Renn, C. J. Jacques, Cori Siri, Mary Jane Jacques, and Tom Giachetti.

Certified Public Accountants (CPAs): Ned Conley and Ken Herrmann.

Risk Management Specialists: Clay Saftner.

Wealth Advisors/Financial Advisors: Patsy DiNuzzo, Michael Kitces, and Ross Levin.

Consultants: Nick Pavlidis, Russ Alan Prince, Matt Lynch, Marty Miller, and Dr. Joseph Bosiljevac.

Professors: Gene Fama Sr., Nobel Laureate; Kenneth French; Ed Lazear (deceased); Robert Novy-Marx; Myron Scholes, Nobel Laureate; Merton Miller, Nobel Laureate (deceased); and Harry Markowitz, Nobel Laureate.

Dimensional Fund Advisors (DFA): David Booth, Rex Sinquefield, James L. Davis, Weston Wellington, Dave Plecha, Dan Wheeler (retired), Dave Butler, Gerard O'Reilly, Joel Hefner, Mike McCann, John Wilson, Daniel Essman, Jewell Ward, John "Mac" McQuown, and Marlena Lee.

Companies/Organizations: Dimensional Fund Advisors (DFA), TD Ameritrade Institutional, Fidelity Institutional, Charles Schwab and Co. Institutional, AICPA, PICPA, and NATP.

And finally, thank you Catherine Turner for your attention to detail in helping me prepare this manuscript for publishing, and to my publisher, Morgan James Publishing, for your continued support behind the scenes to help me share *Don't Get Killed on Taxes* with the people who need it.

Acknowledgments from Steven

My contributions to *Don't Get Killed on Taxes* are a reflection of the incredible people I have had the opportunity to be surrounded by and partner with. So much of what I am able to do is a result of *friends* who have been generous with their professional experience and mentorship throughout my career. In particular, a huge thanks goes to Matthew Jarvis, CFP, President of Jarvis Financial Services, author of *Delivering Massive Value*, cofounder of The Perfect RIA, and cofounder of Retirement Tax Services; and Micah Shilanski, CFP, Partner at Shilanski & Associates, cofounder of The Perfect RIA, and cofounder of Retirement Tax Services. They both set the standard on what it means to have an abundance mentality and Deliver Massive Value™ to everyone around them.

I have also benefited from opportunities to learn from professors, classmates, colleagues, friends, family, and peers along the way. While you have not all been named here, know that I appreciate what you have done.

Foreword

Taxes are universal. They are everywhere and are not going away. Taxes are also necessary. Without taxes, there are no governments, and—in all sincerity—without governments, there is no civilization. But that does not mean you must blindly pay taxes. Many people pay taxes without ever evaluating whether it is possible to pay but pay less.

The reality is that you likely have some control over the amount and when you pay some—if not all—of your taxes. Moreover, if you are like so many people, you are not taking any action to be in control.

The question is very simple . . .

If you were able to legally pay less in taxes, would you?

If you are like almost everyone else, the answer is YES. Yet, there is a high probability you are not taking advantage of all the ways available to you to pay less in taxes. Take a moment to consider what steps you are taking to pay less in taxes. Are you in control?

Legitimately mitigating taxes is a high priority for lots and lots of people. For example, consider successful entrepreneurs. Entrepreneurship is the engine of personal wealth creation the world over. I recently conducted a study of 111 entrepreneurs, all fifty years old or younger, with a net worth (including their businesses) of $50 million or more. In that study, 87.4 percent said that the success of their companies is the way they became personally wealthy. Moreover, they are currently intensely focused on growing their companies, which will add to their personal wealth.

As entrepreneurs become affluent because their businesses are doing well, they can amass wealth outside their companies. All 111 successful entrepreneurs had—on average—investment portfolios of $9.1 million. The monies in their investment portfolios ranged from $1.4 million to $31.7 million. This is clearly a wealthy group of entrepreneurs.

Every successful entrepreneur reported that although they are very interested and attentive to the performances of their investment portfolios, they are much more concerned with mitigating taxes. This was even the case for the entrepreneurs who reported that investing outside their business is the way they became personally wealthy. Consequently, they are readily hiring talented professionals to help them pay less in taxes.

And what most people don't talk about is that the same concepts these ultra-successful people use to legally reduce their tax burden can also help people at virtually all levels of income.

Based on decades of research, it is not only entrepreneurs who desire to pay as little in taxes as legally possible. The ultra-wealthy regularly turn to professionals to help them navigate the tax code. In the aggregate, they pay millions to legally save billions in taxes. For a large percentage of the ultra-wealthy, taking steps to mitigate or eliminate taxes is a top financial priority.

What these successful entrepreneurs and the ultra-wealthy are doing is turning to leading professionals who work with them to examine all possible officially sanctioned ways to pay less in taxes. What it comes down to it, for most people—irrespective of wealth—who want to pay less in taxes and *not* run afoul of the IRS, is being able to work with the appropriate tax experts.

P. J. DiNuzzo and Steve Jarvis have the knowledge and skills to help those in need of tax mitigation and tax strategies evaluate all the options available to them to lower the amount of taxes they owe. They also have the expertise to implement the appropriate tax-saving tactics. And they have the track record to prove it.

These two renowned tax authorities have written the book you are holding to help you understand what you can do to likely pay less in taxes. P. J. and Steve work with people across the wealth spectrum, and they are sharing what most anyone can do to pay the government the minimum possible. That is, they explain a range of actions you can potentially take to put more money in your pocket.

Very importantly, P. J. and Steve dissect the costly myths and provide clarity concerning taxes that lead many to send more money to the IRS than they are legally required to pay. They also provide you with the foundation for developing an effective tax mitigation strategy. I consider their insights to be essential to your long-term financial success.

Again, you do not have to be a successful entrepreneur or ultra-wealthy to benefit from the knowledge they are sharing. To put it bluntly . . . by following their recommendations, you will likely become meaningfully wealthier than you are today.

—Russ Alan Prince, Executive Director, *Private Wealth Magazine*

Introduction:

Why Many People Get Killed on Taxes

I n our combined time working in the world of integrated tax preparation, accounting, financial strategy, and business in general, we've discovered an unfortunate trend: Most people pay way too much in taxes. Maybe you do too.

Taxpayers don't always like to talk about taxes. Some people have a stress headache at the mere mention of the "T" word. Other people feel their blood pressure rising when they realize their annual return is coming up. When it comes to taxes (and perhaps finances in general), they feel out of control and are stuck paying amounts they don't understand.

The message of this book is simple: Even though so many people get killed on their taxes, that doesn't have to be your story. You don't need a degree in business or accounting, or even need to be particularly good at math. You simply need to understand the truth behind many tax misconceptions, then learn the building blocks of what *can* be done to create a plan to reduce your taxes over time.

First, we need to understand the main reasons *why* people get killed on taxes and feel helpless to do anything for the better. It usually boils down to four main situations. Take a look, and see if one or all of them apply to you:

1. They Believe Too Many Tax Myths

In our time helping countless people with their taxes and finances, we've encountered a myriad of myths and misconceptions on the topic. Some of them are oversimplifications of the tax code, some are cop-outs that help people compartmentalize taxes, and others are just poor strategy.

In part 1 of this book, we'll cover the most common myths about taxes we've encountered in our careers. When you look through this section, take the time to really gauge whether you believe some of these myths. They represent a mindset that will hold you back from winning at taxes (and money in general) over your lifetime. In each chapter, we'll also get to the truth, so we can walk into the next section with the correct mindset.

2. They Find Taxes Too Difficult and Complex

Now, don't get us wrong: Taxes are certainly difficult and complex. That's why there's an entire industry of professionals (not to mention software programs) dedicated to helping most of the population navigate their tax return from year to year. In this situation, the word "too" is the operative word.

Taxes are not too difficult or complex for you. The trouble is, you don't necessarily see the smaller pieces and how they fit together. If you did, it would be easier to tackle them. Large and complex problems need to get broken down into smaller pieces. Otherwise, we'll rarely feel the motivation to press forward.

In part 2, we'll go over these basic building blocks. Gaining an understanding of them will give you the tools you need to implement the specific strategies we cover in part 3. Don't gloss over them, even if you feel relatively knowledgeable. You might learn something new that helps you further down the road.

3. They Aren't Familiar with Strategy or Don't Work with Someone Who Is

One of the distinctions we make early and often in this book is the difference between tax *preparation* and tax *strategy*. This is because they represent two entirely different mindsets when it comes to taxes. Do you simply try to get through your tax return with as big of a refund as possible? Or do you treat your annual filing as one tiny piece of an annual tax reduction plan and a lifelong plan to enjoy the smallest tax obligations possible?

You don't have to be born with a silver spoon in your mouth to develop a strong financial strategy. Saving millions in taxes makes the headlines, but nearly everyone can do something to reduce their tax bill if they know what to do. Regardless of your starting point, you can typically build wealth, pay less in taxes than you thought possible, and leave a legacy of inheritance and/or generosity behind.

In part 3, we'll cover twenty of the best strategies to facilitate this. We'll walk into it with the assumption that you have rejected the myths and comprehend the building blocks, and we'll consistently refer to them if you need a refresher. These tactics will give you what you need to thrive when it comes to taxes, retirement, and financial planning.

4. They Look in the Rearview Mirror Instead of through the Front Windshield

Finally, we'll discuss the biggest (and most fatal) mindset we've seen in our careers. People consistently look backward instead of forward when it comes to taxes and finances. They come up with excuses from their past that keep them from moving forward, or they claim that they didn't start life with as many advantages as the next person. At the end of tax season, they look back with relief, wipe the sweat off their brow, and completely forget about taxes again until they see an ad for TurboTax during the Super Bowl.

Instead, they ought to look forward into the rest of their life, and even the lives of their children. The decisions you make about finances this year will have implications when you, your children, your grandchildren, or your heirs are eighty years old, whether you realize it or not. So many people, however, get killed on taxes because they don't do the work to plan this far out. Perhaps it comes from a lack of confidence, or fear of getting it wrong and getting audited ... but they spend their lives feeling out of control when it comes to taxes.

So Here's the Truth

You can navigate the world of taxes successfully. You might not know everything you need to know at the very beginning, but that's okay. You started with a blank slate when it comes to every skill you possess, even the basics like reading and writing. When you gain an understanding of the basics, and then build toward more specific strategies, you'll find things getting simpler. You'll have tax preparers or financial planners saying, "Wow, you really did your homework."

You can make better decisions when it comes to taxes. It doesn't matter what past years have looked like. No matter what your financial picture looks like now, you have an opportunity to make the right decisions in the present—ones that build toward the future.

You don't have to loathe tax season each year. What would your life be like if you felt confident about your financial future? What if you looked forward to tax season each year because it comes as a confirmation that your plans are working? What if you didn't have to get killed on taxes anymore, for the rest of your life?

It doesn't take a ton of initial money. Sometimes it's as simple as making tiny adjustments to withholdings or tax-advantaged investments to get yourself in a better position for next year. Regardless of the tax bracket you find yourself in, there are strategies for you to save money, build wealth, and stop overpaying the IRS.

Lastly, you can take back control. You can become an active participant in your financial life, instead of watching it merely happen to you. In fact, you can become a force to be reckoned with when you understand and apply the right strategies.

Like we touched on before, we'll organize all these concepts into three main parts to equip you with the tools and strategies you need to stop getting killed on taxes.

Part 1 is called Dispelling Tax Myths That Cost You Money. We'll cover the most common myths we hear, analyze exactly why they're wrong, and replace them with the truth. You may identify with some of these myths, and that's okay. We just ask that you read with an open mind and evaluate whether there's a better way.

Part 2 is called Taxes 101: Building Blocks for Effective Tax Strategy. If truth about the myths is the foundation, then these are the basic building materials. Like a contractor understands all their tools and how to use them, you need to gain a grasp of each building block. We'll refer to them consistently throughout the following section.

This final section, part 3, is called Tax Strategies to Avoid Getting Killed on Taxes. We put our heads together to come up with the top twenty strategies taxpayers need to understand in order to owe less in taxes. Though it isn't a hard-and-fast rule, the strategies generally move from more general to more specific. Some of them build upon one another or require an understanding of a previous strategy to successfully implement.

After all is said and done, you won't have to get killed on taxes again, ever. But even better than that, you'll have a firm foundation and solid strategy for the financial future of your dreams. That's the secret: Getting a good understanding of taxes gives you a good understanding of finances at large. When you understand and use these strategies, you'll not only pay Uncle Sam less, but you'll know how to build and maintain generational wealth and write a new destiny for your family tree.

Finally, you will see that we share real-life examples throughout this book to demonstrate how these principles work in real-life. You should know that we have changed the names and certain identifying details in the stories to protect the privacy of the individuals whose stories we reference. Any resemblance of the people referenced to actual persons, living or dead, or actual events is purely coincidental.

Ready to get started?

Part 1:

Dispelling Tax Myths That Cost You Money

There are quite a few myths about taxes circulating. The problem is, they aren't harmless. Believing an incorrect myth about taxes ultimately costs you money. For financial success over the long haul, we need to dispel the myths and determine the truth. This will give us the foundation we need for Part 2: Taxes 101: Building Blocks for Effective Tax Strategy.

We'll break it down into six parts:

➤ Myth #1: "Taxes are a fact. I have no control over how much I pay."

➤ Myth #2: "Paying more in taxes is what I should do."

➤ Myth #3: "As long as I get a refund, I've won."

➤ Myth #4: "I use tax preparation software. I'm all set."

➤ Myth #5: "I have a tax preparer. I'm all set."

➤ Myth #6: "Taking taxes one year at a time is enough, especially because I know my taxes will go down in retirement."

Myth #1:

"Taxes are a fact. I have no control over how much I pay."

et us tell you a story, and you let us know if it starts to sound familiar.

In Steven's tax preparation business, he began working with a married couple who had a relatively normal tax situation. However, taxes stressed them out to no end. This made filing their tax return one of the most stressful times of the year for them.

We know that money can become a huge point of contention in marriages. Different people carry different expectations and practices into their lawfully wedded union ... for better or for worse. So this couple began to experience tension between one another around tax time every year.

Worst of all, sometimes they would file incorrectly or forget important information, and get penalized for it. So on top of the stress they experienced from taxes in general, they had an extra financial barrier to overcome. This, of course, led to more stress.

Does that sound familiar to you at all?

Navigating Tax Fears

Many people, married and single, dread tax season. We let the stress it carries affect our emotions and relationships. Toward the beginning of

9

the year, we can feel it setting in. Maybe we read something on social media about taxes. Perhaps one of the major tax preparation software companies start running ads (we think we counted eight hundred of them airing last Super Bowl). You realize it's that time of year again, and you immediately feel a spike in blood pressure.

So how do we respond? We try to do the minimum to get our taxes filed each year so we can stop thinking about it until next year. Like the married couple mentioned earlier, many of us believe this myth: *Taxes are a fact. I have no control over how much I pay.*

Now, the first part of that statement is verifiably accurate. You can't write at length about taxes without referencing the quote popularly attributed to Benjamin Franklin: "In this world nothing can be said to be certain, except death and taxes."

However, it's important not to conflate the inevitability of taxes with the inability to control how much we pay. In other words, just because tax season always comes doesn't mean we can't control how much we pay. Or *when we pay it.*

The truth is, we can control how much we pay, and most of us can decide when to pay, to some degree. It just feels complicated and arcane on the outside. Some of us are afraid that if we try to change our taxes too much, we'll get audited and/or penalized. Or we'll discover that we owe more than we thought!

However, you don't have to be a rocket scientist (or a Certified Public Accountant (CPA)) to find effective strategies to reduce your tax obligations annually and over your lifetime. It only takes the right knowledge and a little bit of effort on the front end, and most people can end up paying less than they currently do. It also requires a mental shift.

Pivoting Away from Powerlessness

When we tell ourselves that taxes are inevitable, and we can't control how much we pay, then we've forfeited the game before it even starts. It's like a baseball player slamming his bat on the ground and stomping back to the dugout before the pitcher has even thrown a pitch. It's a mindset thing.

You are not powerless when it comes to your taxes. So the first step to taking back control (and not getting killed on taxes) is a mindset shift. You have to decide that you're going to start happening to your taxes, instead of just letting them happen to you, so to speak.

The United States tax code is not just a long list of rules and regulations … It's *a series of choices*. When we don't make the right choices (or any choices, for that matter), we end up paying more in taxes than we need to. When we claim that we can't control our taxes, and do the bare minimum, we usually end up giving the IRS a tidy bonus that we didn't necessarily have to owe.

Also, we wanted to nip this thought in the bud: We're not talking about scheming or trying to game the system. *Don't do that.* We're talking about following the rules and making the right decisions to reduce overall tax obligations. Everyone should absolutely pay the taxes they owe, but there are no patriotic awards for leaving a tip.

There are a few basic ways that you can navigate this series of choices. These become ways you can take back control. We hope you see them and realize that you have a bigger part to play in your taxes than you previously thought.

1. **Withholdings**. These are the amounts withheld on your paycheck if you're an employee (hence the name). You get to decide your withholdings, within certain limitations.
2. **Filing status**. This is the condition that determines your standard deduction, filing requirements, tax rate, and potential credits. Like withholdings, you generally get a choice here.
3. **Qualified accounts**. Most commonly Retirement Savings Accounts, these each have different rules regarding deposits and withdrawals, including deductions for deposits. There are also

unqualified accounts with different rules, presenting another layer of decisions for you to make.

4. **Business structure**. If you ever own a business (even one to manage certain investments), you get to decide the legal structure. Most businesses could fall into two or three categories, each with its own liabilities and tax implications.

5. **Timing of income**. Many people have control over when they're paid. If not, they can certainly control when to sell certain assets and withdraw investments. The timing of income has a greater impact on taxes than some realize.

So right off the bat, we have five choices to make that combine to dramatically affect our yearly obligations and refund. We're more powerful than we realize.

Taking Back Control

As Steven began to work with the married couple, he showed them all this and more. He taught them how to take back control of their taxes, and to stop acting as if they couldn't affect the outcome.

When Steven showed them how to adjust their withholdings to avoid penalties and year-end surprises, they breathed a sigh of relief. Moments like this are why he loves his job. He gets to show people how to take ownership in this area of life and benefit tremendously.

Like this couple, you have a decision to make: Action, or inaction. Fear can keep us in a state of "paralysis by analysis," but choosing not to act is *still a choice*. Put similarly, no decision is a decision.

Taxes are a fact, but you do have control over how much you pay. Dispelling the myth that you have no control is the very first step to long-term success in this arena.

Chapter Summary

Death and taxes are the two most certain things in life, right? And when tax season comes around, we just have to deal with it.

Not quite. Though taxes certainly feel complicated and stressful, there are multiple ways you can control how much you pay. When you put the right series of decisions together, you can significantly lower your lifetime tax obligations.

We talked about a married couple who believed this myth, and how Steven helped them dispel it.

Chapter Takeaways:

✓ When we treat taxes as an uncontrollable fact, they stress us out.

✓ Our tax code is full of *choices*.

✓ Inaction is still a choice.

Myth #2:

"Paying more in taxes is what I should do."

Besides people who view taxes as a fact they have no control over, there are some who agree with that sentiment but even take it a step further. Steven once worked with a single filer who had a different set of preconceptions about taxes. Instead of viewing taxes as something unavoidable and stressful, she mostly thought about taxes as her *duty*.

In other words, she felt she ought to pay a healthy chunk in taxes every year. It was just the right thing to do.

This viewpoint is more common than you might think, especially in a culture where people want to solve social problems and pay things forward. Plus, some people were simply raised with the idea that everybody ought to pay their "fair share" of taxes. So, if someone so much as lifts a finger to pay less, then they're a crook.

In other words, they're getting tax *planning* confused with tax *scheming*. In light of this, we want to consistently affirm that we don't endorse tax scheming whatsoever. We discourage it wholeheartedly. Instead, we want to offer a wholehearted approach whereby someone pays all of their tax obligations with no hook or crook … but not a penny more.

Paying It Forward

There's also a noble twist to this myth. For example, we have worked with some people who are comfortable with high taxes because they want their money to go to social causes funded by tax dollars.

One example comes to mind of an immigrant to the United States. Back when they were getting established here, they received a grant from the government that helped them pay their expenses and get on their feet in their new home country. So they viewed taxes as paying it forward, wanting as much of their money as possible to help other immigrants.

Whether it comes from a certain moral disposition, or because of a desire to help others, this mindset boils down to a simple phrase: *Paying more in taxes is what I should do.*

Now, we don't fully agree with this idea, but that doesn't mean we're Ebenezer Scrooge. We completely support anyone and everyone who chooses to use their hard-earned money to support social causes. That's amazing, and something we should all aspire to.

Less Taxes = More Generosity

We also know that anyone can get their money to go further by *keeping more* at tax time, thus allowing them to support social causes directly. People can fund good causes without using the IRS as the middleman in the relationship. In fact, while some of our taxes go to good causes, not all of it does. Plus, we have no idea how to track where our specific contributions go. And if you are like the immigrant who received a grant here and wishes to pay that forward, you have no control over what the federal government will decide to do with your money.

On top of this, there are no patriotic awards for paying extra to the IRS. You don't get a medal for doing your civic duty in this manner.

So we encourage people to pay exactly what they owe according to the code, with no scheming at all. And no more than that. Then, to carefully select the social causes they want to support and fund them directly.

Let's give an example. If you give $200 to the IRS, it may (or may not) end up giving a portion of that to a social cause you support. Let's say it directs $50 to helping immigrants establish themselves. That's wonderful, but you have no way of knowing that the IRS will continue to do it.

On the other hand, if you give that $200 directly to an organization that helps immigrants, you always know that they're going to get all of that money. Plus, it's a charitable contribution you can deduct on your taxes.

If you consistently work to reduce your tax obligations, you'll free up more money for yourself. Then, you can use that money to contribute to the causes of your choice. Over time, you'll end up doing far more good in this world that way.

It requires proactive planning, though. You still treat taxes as a duty, in a sense, because you always do them on time and with great care. The difference is, you don't start with the mindset that you *ought* to pay more. If anything, you should start with the mindset of owing as little as possible, so that you can give away more.

Chapter Summary

While some people treat taxes as a duty, or simply *the right thing to do*, their noble mindset might be misguided. If a person has fewer tax obligations overall, they can ensure that their money goes directly to their preferred social causes.

We will never encourage any kind of scheming, but we do want to pay the minimum amount of what we owe. This ultimately frees us to do more good in the world than by tipping the IRS.

Chapter Takeaways:

✓ There is no patriotic award for paying more in taxes.

✓ We should pay everything we owe, but not a penny more.

✓ The more money you and I are left with, the more we can *directly* support social causes and people in need.

Myth #3:

"As long as I get a refund, I've won."

Two of Steven's favorite clients of all time were a young married couple who had quite a bit going on in their lives. It was a privilege to help demystify their taxes amid all the life changes they experienced in a short amount of time.

Within the span of one tax year, they had their first child, both finished college, and started their careers. Even one of these represents a huge change to their tax situation! They added a dependent, paid thousands in tuition, and changed jobs. Steven had his work cut out for him.

Before working with him, they had it in mind to get a maximum-sized refund. In their eyes, success looked like getting a huge refund and getting to use it on savings, or a vacation, or some other big purchase they had been eyeing.

One year, they set to work and pulled out all the stops. By the end of tax season, they got $8,500 back!

They felt proud. After all, $8,500 is a *big deal*, especially for young parents at the start of their careers. However, when they told Steven about their refund, it reminded him of a myth so many people believe when it comes to taxes: *As long as I get a refund, I've won.*

No, you haven't. Let's take a step back to explain. We're extremely passionate about this because we believe in tax *planning*. Tax planning is not merely tax *preparation*; it goes a step further. When someone plans their taxes instead of just preparing them year after year, they start thinking with a long-term mindset.

Tax planning is essentially the art of lowering one's lifetime tax obligations. In other words, owing less throughout your life. So, if you could look back at your total IRS bill over your lifetime, it would be *significantly less* than if you hadn't planned.

Attempting to get the maximum refund each year is the antithesis of tax planning! Yet, many people think that if they get a tax refund at all, then they've successfully planned for taxes.

Don't Be Fooled

This is something that the big players in the world of taxes have adopted into their marketing strategy, which possibly explains why so many people fall for it. Just recently, Steven was watching TV and saw an ad spot from H&R Block. Its promise? To get you a big refund.

A good tax planner gets you a big refund. A great tax planner *saves you money*. They do this by minimizing your obligations and helping you pay what you owe as you go, which ends up being far less.

We have to remember this crucial fact: Our tax refunds were *always* our money. When you get a big refund from the IRS, it gives you back something that was legally yours all along.

So your "refund" is simply an *interest-free loan* to the IRS. It holds on to your money for you, puts it to work for the whole year, then gives it back to you … and it feels like winning. But few people do the work to understand how much the IRS kept. Instead, they focus on how much of *their money* the IRS gave back.

So trying to get a large refund is the wrong goal. It was always your money! The only true refunds are tax credits and refundable tax credits.

Those are all well and good, but what you should really focus on is reducing the total tax the IRS keeps at the end.

If your tax preparer is just having you overwithhold on your paycheck so that you get a refund, they might be doing you a disservice. If you withhold a ton of money each year and get a lump sum back around April, you aren't winning.

Most people are just getting their own money back. Few people actually get back from the IRS more than they paid in, through refundable tax credits.

A Mindset Shift

Regarding these young parents who were just starting their careers? Steven showed them that getting a large refund isn't the goal. He advised them to switch up their withholdings and timing of income and tax payments. They learned that lower tax obligations and true tax credits meant more money in their pockets over the long haul.

However, it took switching to a mindset of tax planning. When we plan in this way, we stop looking at our current tax season and begin evaluating our situation with the end in mind. Then, we look for ways to lower the most important number of all: total lifetime obligations.

The rest depends on the goals of the couple or single filer. Some people set as much aside as possible for their retirement and set themselves up with healthy distributions when they retire. Others lower their short-term obligations and use that money to maximize their wealth. Regardless of individual pursuits, they plan their taxes long term and don't treat a large refund as a healthy goal. Over time, they become the real winners.

Chapter Summary

For the married couple mentioned in this chapter, a big tax refund at the end of the season feels like a cause for celebration. The only problem is, they're simply giving an interest-free loan to the IRS, made up of money that was legally theirs all along.

Instead, people should focus on tax planning with their end financial goals in mind, and work from there. This can even result in true refunds in the form of refundable tax credits, but more importantly, money saved long term.

Chapter Takeaways:

✓ Many large tax firms will promise you a large refund each year.

✓ Getting a big refund isn't winning because it was always your money.

✓ To truly win at taxes, you should plan to intentionally lower your total obligations.

Myth #4:

"I use tax preparation software. I'm all set."

Ah, tax preparation software ... It makes good tax planning obsolete, right?

The promise of tax software sounds suspiciously similar to the promise of giant tax preparers. They tell you that you'll get a huge refund, with little to no effort. And, just like the big tax firms, they seem to blast us all with a million ads during NFL playoffs.

A caveat: We have to navigate this area with a bit of nuance because very few strategies are completely good or bad, and this also includes tax tools, like prep software. We don't have to employ black-and-white thinking to this. So let us give tax preparation software its due.

Popular tax preparation software can do a fantastic job of getting the ball rolling when it comes to tax season. Steven is a tax preparer himself. He knows that many people can feel paralyzed when tax time rolls around, and having software handy gives people the practical steps they need to traverse the process.

It also comes with built-in features to help people understand taxes, get a refund, and save them money. So much so, that a huge proportion of people rely on it every year for their filing.

The myth here is *I use tax preparation software. I'm all set.*

Software Alone Will Fail You

This is where nuance comes in. Software is a good thing, but it should never become the tool you completely rely on. This doesn't mean we're asking you to throw it out, but we would encourage you to add checks and balances as well as a healthy dose of tax planning to it.

Using software is no guarantee of success. Even as it becomes more sophisticated year after year, it cannot guarantee you a perfect filing. If you doubt this, just check the fine print conveniently buried in the license agreement. There's a reason that the most popular software products promise you they'll pay the penalty and interest if they get the calculations wrong. Because it happens.

We've heard some horror stories about this.

Once, a popular tax preparation software printed a report showing that a W-2 employee should start making thousand-dollar quarterly estimated tax payments instead of adjusting their withholdings. Not good. See the previous chapter about giving *interest-free loans* to the IRS. Simply put, the software cannot serve you well as a tax advisor. It can only follow subroutines and logic flows to spit out a prewritten suggestion—one that may not apply to your situation.

In another case, Steven saw someone use tax preparation software to apply a certain rule to a year, but he knew that the rule didn't exist yet in that year. When Steven asked them about it, they responded, "The software let me do it, so it must be okay." The worst part? The person he saw using the software incorrectly was a CPA!

So the software doesn't always work the way it was designed to. There's always the danger of human error, even from tax professionals who aren't familiar with the platform (or the tax code, in the above case).

Computers Make Mistakes Too

On top of this, there's machine error.

We've seen plenty of cases where the software will promise a client a certain deduction or credit if they select certain options, only to show the client that those options don't apply in their case. If you're in this situation, and you get audited, the IRS won't care what the software told you.

Frankly, the tax code is *complicated*. That's one of the reasons we often look for something to take care of it for us, like software or a preparer. However, the complexity of the code means that software can't always guarantee that you file correctly—no matter how official the report looks at the end. Plus, even if the software company pays the penalty for you, nobody wants mistakes and amended tax returns on their tax record.

It goes back to the main point we've been talking about throughout part 1: Tax *preparation* has nothing on tax *planning*. Guess which one of those tax preparation software focuses on? Hint: it's in the name.

Software alone is not a substitute for tax *planning*. No matter how sophisticated the technology, it can't sit down with you and discuss your ten-year, twenty-year, or thirty-year plan and generate appropriate action steps. You need the human element for that. Software can't bring empathy, wisdom, or intuition to the table, ever.

So what do we recommend? Well, don't throw the baby out with the bathwater. If you use tax prep software and love it, you have no reason to stop. We simply recommend adding tax planning to the mix. Plus, it wouldn't hurt to have your digital filing checked over by a professional before you hit "Submit." It might just save you the hassle of amending … or worse.

So keep using tax preparation software if it suits you. Just make sure it isn't the only tool in your arsenal.

Chapter Summary

Tax preparation software helps millions of taxpayers every year. It is neither entirely good nor entirely bad as a tool. The problem comes when people treat it as the be-all-end-all.

We've seen a few horror stories of software making life much more difficult for people, and we've even seen newer tax preparers use it incorrectly!

So people should consider adding other tools to the mix, like a seasoned professional to check their work. Additionally, preparation software can't help you with long-term tax *planning*, something we all need if we want to succeed at lowering our tax bill over our lifetime.

Chapter Takeaways:

✓ Tax preparation software is a helpful tool that benefits a huge number of people.

✓ Even so, the software isn't perfect. It can and does fail people.

✓ Consider having a pro check your digital filing, and always consider your long-term tax plan.

Myth #5:

"I have a tax preparer. I'm all set."

This myth is closely related to the previous one, but it gets right to the heart of part 1's theme. Instead of using tax preparation software, some people opt to work with a CPA, Enrolled Agent (EA), or another professional tax preparer for their yearly filing.

This is especially true for those with increasingly complicated tax situations—think about that young married couple who had just graduated from college and had their first child. Additionally, some people opt to bring in an outside accountant when businesses and rental properties come into the mix.

A good preparer is all you need to succeed at taxes for your whole life, right? The thinking goes, *I have a tax preparer. I'm all set.*

Nothing against Tax Pros ...

Don't get us wrong, accountants are wonderful. Steven is a CPA himself. They help demystify taxes, which can feel complex and intimidating for so many people. If you regularly use a tax pro or are considering it, by no means do we discourage you from that. However, we do want to consider what your tax pro can and cannot do for you when it comes to your overall tax strategy.

Tax pros spend most of their time on compliance. They want to file your forms each year and do them correctly. That's essentially where their job starts and stops for the majority of their clientele.

If a tax pro is good, they obsess over getting the details right. They do everything in their power to help you save money and get a sizable refund. Also, they make sure everything gets filed on time.

This takes the guesswork and fear out of tax season, making sure you get it right and avoid pitfalls. There's a reason why many people begin tax season by reaching out to their tax pro.

But very few tax professionals look for proactive tax *planning* opportunities. Your relationship begins and ends during tax season, and it's over once you've filed properly. Thus, most taxpayers only communicate with their tax person a few times a year. This means that your tax pro doesn't coach you about the details, show you what's on the horizon, and help you win over the long haul. They focus on helping you get by, right now.

Preparing versus Planning

As Steven works in this industry, he sees a wide gap between tax professionals and financial advisors. One that we want to help close.

The problem is, most people don't get that level of coaching. For example, did you know that choosing *when* to pay taxes can be a powerful tool in reducing the amount you pay over a lifetime? Most tax pros don't tell their clients to pay taxes until tax season rolls around again. In this situation, you aren't losing anything. You're just missing out on the opportunity to save more money over time. But the fact that the pain isn't so obvious means that people often miss it. They aren't even aware of the problem they have.

One preparer that Steven talked to explicitly said, "I never tell a client to pay taxes before they absolutely have to." So, even in situations where the client could pay less over their lifetime, they don't because their tax pro didn't make them aware of their options. Ouch.

This lack of forward-thinking costs the client in the long run, even if they think they're winning by getting a sizable refund. It's like tax tunnel vision.

Again, it's good to have someone who focuses on the current year and prepares your taxes correctly. It's not a knock against tax pros. But you also need to plan for the future, transcending the situation right in front of you and helping you win over a lifetime.

Here are a few questions you should ask yourself (or your professional) to make sure you are being taken care of:

1. Are you on a mass production conveyor belt? Does your preparer really know you beyond a few details from your file? You should work with someone willing to take the time to learn about your life and long-term goals, and willing to help you get there. If a tax preparer alone can't provide you with that, consider adding a financial planner to the mix.

2. Do you have a timely tax planning meeting with your tax pro? One that occurs outside your yearly filing time? If they simply want to rush to get this year's filing done and then move on, that's a red flag.

3. Do you have professionals around you who care about your overall lifetime financial prosperity? Again, this isn't a call to abandon your preparer because they can't be everything to you. It's an invitation to get whoever and whatever you need to win at finances long term. It takes planning in addition to preparation.

Remember, tax pros are fantastic. But don't assume you're all set because you use one!

Chapter Summary

Much like tax preparation software, people tend to over-rely on their accountant for their taxes. This can create a situation where the responsibility is more or less outsourced.

While CPAs and other accountants are fantastic resources, they often do not provide you with help toward your lifetime tax strategy. This frequently causes short-term gains but long-term losses.

Someone on your financial team needs to be responsible for tax planning. If that's not you personally, consider adding a financial planner or tax advisor to the mix to ensure you win at taxes (and finances in general) over your lifetime.

Chapter Takeaways:

✓ Many people hand off responsibility for their taxes to a tax pro when tax season comes, and then try not to think about taxes for the rest of the year.

✓ Tax pros are a good thing, but they focus on compliance rather than strategy.

✓ We should make sure our tax preparers know and care about us, and potentially fill in the strategy gap with other advisors.

Myth #6:

"Taking taxes one year at a time is enough, especially because I know my taxes will go down in retirement."

L et us tell you the story of an engineer Steven worked with. This man worked as a W-2 employee for his entire career, with no extra bells and whistles (taxwise) except for a couple of rental properties later on. It goes without saying that preparing his taxes each year didn't take much effort.

Also, throughout his career, he contributed to a Retirement Savings Account (RSA). He had enough put away that he could afford to live off his Required Minimum Distributions (RMDs) for the rest of his life.

Simple, right? He made it. He did everything we're supposed to do when it comes to taxes and savings, and now he could enjoy relaxing on the beach, catching up on his reading, and maybe adopting a hobby or two.

Well, not quite. Yes, he got to retire, but things most certainly didn't stay simple. He was immediately surprised by all the choices he had to start making regarding his financial and tax life.

Why? For one, when his RMD started hitting, he got bumped up a tax bracket. Ouch. That's never an enjoyable event, but it was made worse by the fact he had just walked away from his main source of income.

Thinking Ahead

While this engineer did things right year by year, he didn't think too far ahead. And that's what ended up hurting him. Whether he realized it or not, he acted from this mindset: *Taking taxes one year at a time is enough, especially because I know my taxes will go down in retirement.*

Neither of those statements works out in reality. Taking taxes one year at a time is not enough if you want to ensure you set yourself up for retirement (or even leave a legacy). Plus, taxes don't always go down in retirement. In our experience, they typically don't.

If you've done well to plan your retirement, and you've saved a chunk of money, then don't assume your overall income will drop after you retire. For many people, like our engineer, it actually goes up. This is especially true because many people begin saving for retirement later than they should, and they put away a huge proportion of their income during the latter half of their career.

Generally speaking, when your income increases, your taxes will too. Plus, RSAs have rules about how much you need to (or can) withdraw and when the money is taxed, and they come with various fees and penalties if you get it wrong.

Additionally, taxes almost never go down in general. Think of it this way: Tax rates can only do one of three things. They can go up, they can stay the same, or they can go down. That's it.

So ask yourself, are you worried tax rates will go down?

Assuming that taxes will go down is a losing bet. Over the course of your lifetime, have tax rates in general, and the taxes you pay personally, gone up or down? What makes you think it will be different for your retirement?

The fact that taxes tend to increase forms one factor. The other factor comes from retiring itself.

When we retire, it naturally shuffles our sources of income. Typically, our main source of income comes from a W-2 or 1099, and when we retire, that goes away. Now our main source of income comes from our retirement savings or gains from other investments. When your income gets more complex, your tax situation gets more complex too.

Another factor: Many people move when they retire. Different states (or even countries) have different tax rules. But how many of us have taken the time to understand how moving to Arizona or Florida (or the retirement spot of our choice) will affect our tax situation?

Save Yourself a Headache

Thankfully, you have the ability to prepare now, whether retirement feels like a far-off dream or it's less than a year away. Here are two things you can do to prepare yourself:

1. Don't assume things will get simpler. Instead, educate yourself.

The first step involves your mindset. Your tax situation will probably not get simpler when you retire. It certainly won't be simpler the first year while you make adjustments to your income, plan distributions, and potentially move.

Regardless of whether you face more or less complexity, you can educate yourself now, so you're ready when the day comes. Talk to a professional who understands the importance of tax and retirement planning. As any retired person will tell you, the day is coming faster than you think.

2. Begin planning now, even your potential destination.

You have to make choices about how, when, and where you pay taxes if you want to win over your lifetime. That includes planning into your retirement days.

Do you know what your sources of income will be once you retire? Do you know where you plan to live and how it will affect your taxes?

You don't need to have an exact plan as far as income sources, the amount they will net you, or your precise geographical location decades from now. But you should have an idea. It could help to make a list of top destinations and take the time to learn about their tax rules. Additionally, you should know whether your savings and investments will support you once you clock off for the last time.

Don't just take it year by year, and don't assume that your financial life will get simpler once you retire.

Busting the Myths

What happened to the engineer from the beginning of the chapter? He's all right, by the way. However, if he had known what his RMDs would do to his tax situation, chances are he would have either found a different RSA or diversified his investments. Plus, he could have saved himself a headache at the beginning of the most highly anticipated season of his life, and ended up paying less overall in taxes, had he begun thinking about all of this earlier.

These were the main myths that we encounter when talking to people about taxes. If there are any that you've believed up until now, we encourage you to reconsider. The heart of the matter is this: We all need to *plan* for our taxes, instead of just preparing them year in and year out. If we do this, we can lower our lifetime obligations, retire in style … and not get killed on taxes.

 ## Chapter Summary

Taxes tend to increase instead of staying the same or going down. Our tax situation changes when we switch our source of income or move to a different state. Even though both of those statements are true, many people still assume that taxes will get simpler when they retire.

Also, people often just take their taxes as they come each year, and never think too far ahead. This could be due to the stress that taxes bring, or the false idea that taxes will decrease or get simpler when retirement comes.

Instead, we should start our lifetime tax plan right now, which includes our retirement. If we prepare adequately, retiring won't be a headache but a joyful moment capping off our career and financial plan.

Chapter Takeaways:

✓ Many people never think about taxes unless it's tax season.

✓ Plenty of people assume that taxes will decrease and get simpler when they retire.

✓ We all should start planning now for our retirement, so we know what to expect, and so we can lower our lifetime tax obligations.

Part 2:

Taxes 101: Building Blocks for Effective Tax Strategy

———————————

I hope you see now the importance of having a tax strategy. We should plan for the long term, not just avoid thinking about taxes until the annual deadline, only to rush to prepare a tax return and then have them drop out of our mind again.

But what constitutes a good tax strategy?

We've started with a proper foundation of truth. Now we need the basic building blocks to really move things forward. We're going to talk about the five primary building blocks of an effective tax strategy, a strategy that helps you lower your tax obligation over your lifetime.

It might seem complicated at the outset, so we want to break it down into manageable chunks. We'll outline each of the five building blocks and how to implement them:

➤ Building Block #1: Managing Brackets and Rates; Marginal vs. Effective Tax Rates

➤ Building Block #2: Optimizing Tax-Deferred and Tax-Free Investing Opportunities

➤ Building Block #3: Timing and Planning Your "Paycheck" for the Rest of Your Life

➤ Building Block #4: Getting Intentional with *Where* You Pay Taxes

➤ Building Block #5: Having a System to Capture Every Benefit You're Entitled To

Building Block #1:

Managing Brackets and Rates; Marginal vs. Effective Tax Rates

"What's my tax bracket?"

A common (and good) question to ask ... but like many questions, the answer is, "It depends."

First, for those unacquainted, what is a tax bracket?

At the federal level (which will be our primary focus), not all income is taxed at the same rate. The tax code is progressive, meaning that as income increases, the tax rate on each new dollar of income also increases. The tax rate for your next dollar of income is commonly referred to as your tax bracket. These brackets are liable to change each year, so they're worth checking. By the way, the brackets get further delineated by the filing status of the taxpayer. So there's a bracket for single filers, married filing separately, married filing jointly, head of household, and qualifying widow(er).

Let's use the status of married filing jointly as an example because it relates to a couple of stories on this topic. For taxes paid in 2022, the first several categories for income tax were

1. $0 to $20,550 (10 percent)
2. $20,551 to 83,550 (12 percent)

3. $83,551 to $178,150 (22 percent)
4. $178,151 to $340,100 (24 percent)
5. $340,101 to $431,900 (32 percent)
6. $431,901 to $647,850 (35 percent)
7. Over $647,850 (37 percent)

Most filers will find their total household income falling into one of these categories.

Additionally, tax brackets are progressive. This means that when you find yourself in a higher tax bracket, you don't pay that bracket's tax rate for your entire income. You pay that rate for the income above the lower threshold of the bracket.

Let's use an example to make it clearer.

One married couple Steven worked with made $80,000 altogether and filed jointly. Therefore, they paid 10 percent for the first $20,550 and 12 percent for the rest.

This illustrates the difference between marginal tax rate and effective tax rate, terms you will hear from time to time. Knowing the difference will help you understand how to better manage your taxes and come out ahead.

The marginal tax rate is the amount of tax a person will pay on their *next dollar* of income. So, if they have a marginal rate of 10 percent, then they earn a dollar, they'll need to send ten cents to Uncle Sam. So that married couple? When they went from $20,550 earned, on their 20,551st dollar, their marginal tax rate went from 10 percent to 12 percent. Every dollar after that had a marginal rate of 12 percent.

Your effective tax rate is how much you *actually pay in total*. This is usually lower than your top marginal tax rate. Let's do the math on that $80,000 the couple earned.

> $20,550 ´ 0.10 = $2,055 for their first bracket. They earned $59,450 more than that, though, to get to $80,000. All that income fell into the next bracket up:
>
> $59,450 ´ 0.12 = $7,134 for the rest of their income. If we add that together, their total income tax would be $9,189. Now, to determine their effective tax rate, we divide that number by their income.
>
> $9,189 ¸ $80,000 = 0.1148. If you multiply that number by one hundred, you get the percentage of their effective tax rate, about 11.5 percent.

So why does all that math matter? It matters because you can lower your taxable income in order to slide yourself into a lower tax bracket, thus paying a fair amount less in taxes. The lower your taxable income, the lower your effective tax rate will be.

In this section, we have been describing the tax rates for *ordinary* income, but not all income is created equal for tax purposes. There are separate tax brackets that apply to long-term capital gains and qualified dividends.

Qualified Income Brackets (Long-Term Capital Gains and Qualified Dividends)

Capital gains are the profits[1] you make from the sale of assets: stocks, bonds, real estate, coins, and cryptocurrency, to name several, that you have held for at least a year before selling. Qualified dividends are typically dividends paid by US companies or qualifying foreign companies on stock you have owned for a specific period of time (at least sixty days, but longer in certain situations).

Like ordinary income, qualified income is broken up into brackets depending on your filing status and the amount of *total* taxable income

---

1   In the simplest terms, profit is the difference between how much one paid for an asset and how much one sold it for, although there can be other factors to consider.

you've made overall during the tax year. The 2022 tax brackets for a married couple filing jointly were:

1. $0 to $83,350 = 0 percent
2. $83,351 to $517,200 = 15 percent
3. $517,201+ = 20 percent

These brackets also use a progressive system, like ordinary income taxes. In fact, your qualified income *adds to your ordinary income to determine your total taxable income* (not everyone remembers this). So that impressive 0 percent for $83,350 feels less impressive when you're like the couple we mentioned before and already have $80,000 in ordinary taxable income. This would mean that their first $3,350 of capital gains would have the 0 percent tax rate, but not the rest.

However, there's an important distinction: If you buy the asset and sell it for a profit within the same year (twelve-month period, not calendar year), it counts as *ordinary income* instead of qualified income for tax purposes. So, when tax time comes around, your short-term capital gains simply add on to your total taxable income and are taxed accordingly.

So for a taxpayer in the highest ordinary income tax bracket (earning over $539,900 if single or over $647,850 if married filing jointly) with $10,000 in capital gains, this distinction could be the difference between paying only $2,000 in taxes (qualified income) or $3,700 in taxes (ordinary income).

Also, there are significant exceptions for certain types of assets and investments. These include a higher capital gains tax rate for gains on collectible assets like precious metals and coins and Net Investment Income Tax owed by certain high earners.

Here's an important example:

The couple we mentioned who made $80,000 in one year? They wanted to go ahead and sell large stock holdings that year too. They thought that their capital gains would be taxed at $0 because their income was less than $83,350. See their mistake? They didn't realize that capital gains taxes are progressive, and that they add on to your total taxable income.

If they made $80,000 in income, and then made a profit of, say, $10,000 on sold stock holdings, then their total taxable income would be $90,000. That's $6,650 over the first capital gains threshold of $83,350. So the first $3,350 of that $10,000 would get the 0 percent tax rate. The rest, $6,650, would get the 15 percent tax rate, for a total of $997.50 in capital gains taxes on top of their $9,189 in income tax.

It would be even worse if they had bought those stocks in the same year they sold them because then they would simply count as income. Their total taxable income would be $90,000, and it would use the income tax brackets (12 percent until $83,550 and 22 percent for the rest) instead of the capital gains tax brackets. So the first $3,550 would have a rate of 12 percent and the next $6,450 would have a rate of 22 percent for a total of $1,845.

Putting It All Together

We know that may sound complex at the first read. What it means practically is that taxpayers should do a few things to take control of their brackets and tax rates:

1. Understand How Long You've Held an Asset Before You Sell it

As you can see in the story above, the couple would have to pay about $850 more if their stocks were held for less than one year. There will absolutely be times when selling an asset before twelve months is the right decision, but don't make the classic mistake of deciding when to sell without understanding the tax piece.

2. Pay Attention to Total Taxable Income After Asset Sales

Your net capital gains will raise your total taxable income and be taxed progressively. If your total taxable income is less than a certain amount

($83,350 in 2022) you're in the clear. If not, you may get hit with far more taxes than you were expecting.

3. Balance Your Ordinary Income and Qualified Income

The ideal scenario in terms of effective tax rate? Your total taxable income is less than the capital gains tax threshold, which is currently (for 2022) $83,350 for married couples filing jointly and $41,675 for single filers. However, many single people and households exceed those rates, which isn't bad in itself. More income means more income, after all.

However, you can balance your income and capital gains somewhat by putting your income into investments and Retirement Savings Accounts, which lowers your taxable income before capital gains get added. This could end up saving you thousands of dollars in taxes if you do it right, which we'll cover more in-depth in part 3.

4. Pay Attention to the Rules for Each Kind of Income

Finally, as hinted at previously, different investments have different tax rules. Some capital gains, like collectible assets, have a higher tax rate. Other investments have rules about when you pay taxes on them.

Another couple Steven worked with learned this the hard way. They sold stocks they owned during the year, and then waited until tax filing season to pay the taxes on them. The problem? The IRS expected those taxes to be paid during the quarter of the sale.

This led to thousands of dollars in unexpected taxes, which nobody wants. To add insult to injury, they also had hundreds of dollars in underpayment penalties.

Think of it like backing up when you're driving. One of the first things they teach you in driver's education is to look behind you whenever you reverse, with your mirror or by turning your actual head if possible. For most drivers, it becomes a reflex. The same should go for your income. Whenever you have money coming in, get in the habit of asking,

"What does that mean for my taxes?"

So ends our crash course on income tax brackets, capital gains, and marginal and effective tax rates. At the end of the day, your goal is to have the lowest effective tax rate for your total taxable income over your lifetime. (More to come on the "lifetime" piece of this. Having a long-term strategy instead of a "this year" strategy is one of the most effective tools to avoid getting killed on taxes.)

Chapter Summary

The question "What's my tax bracket?" often has another question beneath it: "What's my overall tax rate?" This can be calculated by paying attention to the brackets for income tax and capital gains for your tax year, and doing a bit of math.

Remember that your total taxable income comes from the addition of your net capital gains to your taxable income, and that both brackets are progressive, adding to a sum total that dictates your capital gains tax rate.

If you hold onto assets for longer than one year, pay attention to your total taxable income, and seek to fill up (but not exceed) your capital gains bracket with your total taxable income, you'll be in a good position for a low effective tax rate.

Chapter Takeaways:

✓ There are two main tax brackets: income tax and capital gains tax.

✓ You will be taxed progressively on your income according to the income tax bracket, then your net capital gains will be added and taxed progressively to determine your grand total.

✓ Get in the habit of looking at the tax rules for each kind of income you have coming in to avoid nasty surprises.

Building Block #2:

Optimizing Tax-Deferred and Tax-Free Investing Opportunities

What is the single largest expense you will face in retirement?

Some reading this might assume that it will be buying a new house in the retirement destination of their choosing. Perhaps others have had their eye on a dream car that they've been waiting to drive. Others may think that the tour of Europe they've been planning for decades will eat into their savings more than anything else.

For the most part, all of these answers are incorrect. Time and time again in Steven's experience helping people understand taxes in retirement, he's seen people believe myths (or completely not think) about taxes.

It turns out that for most people he's worked with, taxes themselves end up becoming the largest expense folks face in retirement. However, few people truly take the time to understand their opportunities when it comes to retirement saving and plan accordingly. Even fewer set up their retirement savings in a way that lessens their overall tax liability and gives them a fund for other large expenses.

Remember the engineer from Myth #6 who retired and found his tax rate going up? His story also illustrates another important point: on top of that unexpected expense, he had to take into account the prospect of moving to a desired location or taking the trip of a lifetime to celebrate the end of his career.

Expect Unexpected Expenses

Like him, everyone will experience moments in their lives where they need a large sum of money, all at once. It's unavoidable. Now, hopefully, these large sums are needed for good reasons. Perhaps you want to buy an RV or take an amazing trip with your family. Or one day you decide it's finally time to take everyone to Disneyland.

However, life happens. Most of the time when we have a large unexpected expense, it's tied to an emergency or tragedy. It comes in the form of a large medical expense or funeral cost. Someone in our life has a crisis, and we have to pack up and go to them. Or a disaster strikes that isn't exactly covered by our insurance policy.

Either way, you end up needing a chunk of change, and fast. Many people simply don't have access to that kind of money. This could be due to a lack of planning, or because they put it into a bucket that they don't have full access to until they're 59½ years old.

Now, we know that thought may give rise to some anxiety in you, depending on your current situation. That's not our intention. We want to give you the opportunity to plan ahead and take surprise expenses in stride.

How much better would you feel to know that you had a bucket of money that you could use without paying *any* taxes at the time you need the money?

Also, as mentioned earlier, *taxes don't always go down when you retire*. Especially when you've done everything "right," and invested into a tax-deferred account every year to minimize your tax obligations during your career. When you begin withdrawing, it could very likely bump you up a tax bracket or two … especially if you were maximizing your tax-deferred contributions.

So how do we build that bucket?

It requires understanding the two main types of Retirement Savings Accounts (RSAs) and leveraging the benefits of tax-exempt accounts.

Here's the breakdown:

Tax-Deferred Accounts

Tax-deferred accounts are RSAs that allow you to postpone paying the taxes on your contributions until you eventually retire and begin withdrawing from that account. They are most commonly 401(k)s and Individual Retirement Accounts (IRAs). These accounts lower your tax bill now, but the IRS is only so patient.

For 401(k)s, at the time of this writing, individuals can contribute up to $20,500 yearly to them if they're under fifty years old, and $27,000 yearly if they're fifty years old or older, and that's just the employee portion! Including employer matching, profit sharing, or other contributions, a total of $61,000 can be contributed annually if they're under fifty years old, and $67,500 if they're fifty years old or older. For IRAs, it's $6,000 for forty-nine and below, and $7,000 for fifty and up.

There are other rules that are important to understand to figure out just how much a person or couple can contribute, including how much earned income they have, but the amounts above reflect the maximum possible contributions.

Pro Tip

An often missed opportunity is the fact that you can potentially contribute the max in a year to *both* a 401(k) and an IRA. They are not mutually exclusive.

Note: The rules about contribution limits can change from year to year, which leads us to perhaps the most important point of this section: *The IRS can and will change the rules of the game.*

Remember, the taxes on your IRA are due when the money is withdrawn. This often happens when you're retired, due to the early withdrawal penalty that kicks in when you withdraw while less than 59½ years old.

As we mentioned before, taxes can either go down, stay the same, or go up. What has happened to them during your and my lifetime? What will they most likely do before you retire? We're not Nostradamus, but we have a hunch that the rules will change at least a few more times before that day comes … and likely not in a way that benefits the taxpayer.

Steven sometimes refers to it as the "IRS Mortgage." Your 401(k) or IRA may have a balance of $500,000, but there is a potential huge cost to withdrawing that money. Unlike a traditional mortgage, Congress can vary the rate at any time. In fact, these terms are completely up to the "mortgage" holder. So the IRS does allow us to defer the taxes on our savings … but it makes no commitment on how much we'll be charged in the future. After all, the tax code is written in pencil.

This makes it virtually impossible to know which retirement tax bracket you'll end up in. So you do have a choice over when you pay your taxes, but only if you pay taxes right now do you know for sure how much you'll pay.

Only in very special circumstances would you buy a house where the mortgage holder can arbitrarily change the terms. The same should go for these sorts of accounts.

However, there's a caveat: Tax-deferred accounts are great. We're not saying they're awful, and tax-exempt accounts are even better! Tax-deferred accounts work for so many people. They are able to lower their taxable income in the present by contributing, which incentivizes planning for the future. Plus, the fact that they penalize early withdrawals can be a blessing in disguise. It motivates people to hold on to their savings for longer and let them grow.

That being said, tax-exempt accounts have a few advantages:

Tax-Exempt (Roth) Accounts

Tax-exempt accounts require you to pay the taxes on your contributions here and now, and then your withdrawals in the future are all tax-free (with a few limitations on timing). So you have to still pay taxes on your income before you put the money in, but all the growth happens tax-free.

The two most common tax-exempt accounts are the Roth IRA, and the at times neglected Roth 401(k). Sometimes people see the "401(k)" in the name and assume that it has the same rules as the traditional 401(k). But the word "Roth" is the keyword here. They're named after William Roth, a senator from Delaware who helped put the Roth IRA into law in 1998.

Long story short, if it's a Roth, it grows with $0 tax liability but doesn't count toward your tax deductions when you contribute. Is that worth it? For most people, the answer is absolutely.

In a tax-exempt account, Congress can no longer change the rules of the game on you.[2] It can't play the role of mortgage holder in this situation. It simply collects taxes on your earned income that you used to fund the account. Once you turn 59½, all of your distributions become tax-free. This includes your contributions and all of your growth.

Not only that, but if you ever need to, you can withdraw your contributions without *any* taxes or penalties. You will, however, get taxed on the *gains* if you withdraw early and potentially pay a penalty depending on your age. That is, unless you're withdrawing for a first-time home purchase, education expenses, and a couple of other qualifiers.

Roth vs. Traditional

Steven once had a client who we'll call Bob. He expressed something that demonstrates the mindset of many people when it comes to retirement

---

2   We mentioned already that the tax code is written in pencil, and that is absolutely the case. It is possible that Congress could make wholesale changes to the Roth rules beyond increasing tax rates (which is what we are really talking about when we tout the advantages of Roth), but this has been politically unpopular and seems unlikely.

savings funds. Steven asked him what he'd do in the case of a huge surprise expense. This is a standard question for financial planners, and it often reveals quite a bit.

Bob said, "I have $200,000 in my 401(k), so anything less than that, and I'm good."

Not quite, Bob. He had a traditional 401(k), not the Roth, meaning that any withdrawals would be taxed after contributing to his total taxable income. Not only that, if Bob were under 59½, then he'd also get penalized for the distribution.

He'd probably be looking at something closer to $150,000 or $160,000, depending on the other income he made that year.

Bob isn't alone. Too often, we encounter taxpayers treating their traditional retirement funds like a bank account. If you have a $200,000 401(k) or IRA, you don't actually have $200,000.

But if that money is in a Roth IRA or Roth 401(k), the outlook is better. Bob could withdraw any of his previous contributions with no penalties or taxes. There are even circumstances where he could withdraw the growth if he had to. Plus, once he's 59½ and has had the account at least five years, all of his distributions are tax- and penalty-free, forever.

This is important for your expectations. This knowledge doesn't change your income or the amount of money you have access to today. But it does give you the choice to adjust.

How Should I Balance My Investing Opportunities?

The first step is to understand your tax situation long-term. Everyone starts with different taxable income, investments, and accounts. Some people work for an employer that offers benefits in the form of contribution matching or better tax deductions for contributions. Others already have a significant tax-deferred account and need to decide what to do with it.

This could involve talking to a CPA or financial planner. Steven always works with clients to understand what their tax rate is now and what it might be in the future to help them understand their options. However, current tax information and rules are available for free, online. Again, the IRS reserves the right to change the rules at any time, meaning the situation could change for income, capital gains, and tax-deferred accounts. But regardless, one can get a general idea.

Next, if someone expects their tax rate to be the same or higher in retirement, they should begin contributing the maximum amount to a Roth IRA. They could also contribute to a Roth 401(k) if their workplace allows. They should also review the possibility of converting their tax-deferred account to a Roth IRA.

For some, however, they may review their current situation and realize that nothing needs to change. This could be in the case where they're in a higher tax bracket now than they will be when they retire, and they're confident they'll stay that way. Or they could already be maxing out their Roth IRA and need other investing opportunities. In other cases, the taxpayer's Modified Adjusted Gross Income (MAGI) is too high for them to invest in a Roth IRA in the typical manner. We'll review all that and more later in the book.

We'll leave you with this, here: If you think that tax rates will go down, and the IRS won't change the rules during your lifetime, then you have nothing to worry about with a traditional IRA or 401(k) account. If you think tax rates will stay the same or rise, you may want to think about moving some of your money into a tax-exempt account.

Chapter Summary

There are key differences between tax-deferred and tax-exempt Retirement Savings Accounts, chief among them being the moment the taxpayer is required to pay taxes. Tax-deferred accounts are taxed at the moment of withdrawal, but the flip side is that contributions count as a reduction in taxable income when they are made. Tax-exempt accounts don't confer this bonus at the time of contribution, but the distributions are tax-free, including any growth along the way.

Taxpayers need to balance their contributions based on their situation. This includes their income, employer, current investments, age, and more. However, in many situations there is a benefit to contributing the maximum amount to a Roth IRA, and even considering converting tax-deferred accounts to tax-exempt accounts.

When you contribute to a tax-free retirement account, it helps you pay the minimum amount in taxes after you retire, or sometimes none at all. Plus, it serves as a rainy day or emergency fund that doesn't penalize you for qualified distributions.

Chapter Takeaways:

✓ Though few truly do, it's important to understand the difference between tax-deferred and tax-exempt retirement accounts.

✓ The Roth IRA, a tax-exempt retirement account, has some of the most beneficial rules for taxpayers, including tax-free distributions once the taxpayer meets certain criteria related to their age and the age of the account.

✓ Effective tax planning considers the long term, not just what results in the lowest tax bill now.

Building Block #3:

Timing and Planning Your "Paycheck" for the Rest of Your Life

Remember Bob, from the previous chapter? He had $200,000 in a traditional 401(k). At the moment, the IRS can't tax this money. He's been steadily contributing to this account throughout his career and getting a deduction to his taxable income from his contributions. This has lowered his effective tax rate throughout most of his life, and as we saw in the previous chapter, has given him a bit of overconfidence when it comes to his total savings.

Let's say that Bob kept contributing to his 401(k) throughout his career to the point where he contributed $500,000 overall. The investments would also likely grow and generate tax-deferred income, so for the sake of easy numbers, let's say he has $1,000,000 in this account by the time he retires.

Now, since he only gets taxed when he withdraws from the account, he can just withdraw the bare minimum he needs for his lifestyle and keep taxes low, right?

Yes and no. It's true that he gets taxed when he withdraws. In fact, from here on out, his distributions will count as taxable income to the IRS and be taxed according to the brackets we covered in Building Block

#1. Wanting to pay less in taxes feels like a universal truth (at least for the clients Steven works with), so most people are interested in keeping taxes as low as possible each year.

However, there's another spanner in the works, called Required Minimum Distributions (RMDs).

Think of it this way: The IRS is only so patient. Bob has been tucking hundreds of thousands of dollars away throughout his career, and so far hasn't had to pay a cent in taxes for that money. The IRS realizes that Bob could save a ton of money by only withdrawing a tiny amount each year, and potentially avoid paying taxes on some or maybe even all of it.

But as we know, death and taxes are the only certainties in life. The IRS devised a way to collect what it feels is its due, and so RMDs came into existence.

An RMD is what it sounds like. When you reach a certain age, you *must* withdraw a certain amount from your tax-deferred retirement account, or face penalties. These accounts include but are not limited to 401(k)s, traditional IRAs, and SIMPLE IRAs (which stands for **S**avings **I**ncentive **M**atch **PL**an for **E**mployees and lets employers and employees contribute to traditional IRAs set up for the employees).

When you withdraw that RMD, it counts toward your taxable income, and you have to pay taxes on it during your yearly tax filing.

How RMDs Work

At the time of this writing, RMDs kick in when the taxpayer turns seventy-two. So on April 1 of the year after Bob's seventy-second birthday, he'll have to withdraw a portion of his, and keep doing so every year. Now, sometimes a person can delay the start of RMDs if they're still working, depending on their retirement plan. However, if someone is both retired and above seventy-two, RMDs will apply for all the aforementioned retirement accounts.

Additionally, Bob can withdraw more than his RMD each year if he so chooses. That's why it's called the required *minimum*. It becomes the floor of what Bob takes out every year, and again, it gets taxed as ordinary income with very few exceptions.

How are RMDs calculated? Like most things in the world of taxes, it depends. RMD amounts depend on the value of the account and the age of the taxpayer. They also have different rules depending on marital status, spouse's age, and inheritance status.

Generally speaking, you take the Fair Market Value of the account (essentially the balance on your statement at December 31) and divide it by a *factor* found on the IRS website that roughly corresponds to the age of the taxpayer vs. their life expectancy as decided by the IRS. The idea is to make RMDs a portion of the total value of the account, proportional to each year the taxpayer has left to live.

If you don't take your RMD, you will incur a steep penalty that you'll need to pay no matter what. This is 50 percent of the amount you chose not to withdraw, which is always higher than the amount you'd be taxed if you had withdrawn the money.

An Example

How much will Bob's RMD be?

Let's assume that he had $1,000,000 in his account on December 31, 2021, and also turned seventy-two that year.

This $1,000,000 would be divided by a factor number based on his age. There are three situations for determining factor numbers, found in IRS Publication 590-B:[3]

1. Bob has a spouse who is ten or more years younger than him and is named as the sole beneficiary of the account. In this instance, he would use Table II.

---

3   U.S. Department of the Treasury, Internal Revenue Service, *Publication 590-B: Distributions from Individual Retirement Arrangements (IRAs)*, (Washington, DC: 2022), https://www.irs.gov/pub/irs-pdf/p590b.pdf.

2. Bob is actually inheriting the account. In this case, he'd use Table I.
3. Bob is unmarried, or his spouse is nine years younger than him or less, or he has multiple beneficiaries. Here (the most common scenario), he'd use Table III.

Since Bob is seventy-two, and he's using Table III, his factor is 27.4. If you divide $1,000,000 by 27.4 you get $36,496.35, his RMD for the 2021 tax year. The next year, his RMD may be more or less, depending on how much more he chooses to withdraw, and how much the account appreciates.

RMDs, Social Security, and Medicare

As you can see, RMDs increase your total taxable income. This could be in addition to other sources of income, like rental income or capital gains from taxable investments. Your income also affects other benefits when you retire, like how much Social Security you receive and how much you pay for Medicare Part B (before Medicare starts it also affects the amount of tax credit you are eligible for if you purchase healthcare from the marketplace), among others. This is extremely important to be aware of since it could take away from vital sources of income you expect when you retire.

How do RMDs impact Social Security? Well, Social Security benefits aren't taxed if your income falls below a certain threshold—$25,000 for a single earner and $32,000 for married filing jointly in 2022. When your RMDs begin, they may push you over the threshold, requiring you to pay taxes on your Social Security benefits. If you're married and earn over $44,000, you may have to pay tax on 85 percent of your Social Security benefits.

"But Medicare doesn't show up on my tax return, how would RMDs affect Medicare?" The amount you pay for Medicare Part B is determined based on your Modified Adjusted Gross Income, or MAGI (for many taxpayers this is equal to line 11 of the 2021 IRS Form 1040, although there are other considerations). As income goes up, you may have to pay higher premiums for your Medicare coverage, potentially thousands of dollars more each year. As we've been discussing, RMDs will inevitably push your income up in most situations.

If you have more specific questions, it may be worthwhile to sit down with an expert.

How to Reduce the Taxes on Your RMDs

While RMDs are required, that doesn't mean we have to sit back and just wait for RMDs to happen. There are ways to anticipate them and lower your tax obligations on them, just like with regular income.

1. Consider Tax-Free Investment Opportunities

With the knowledge of RMDs and how they will influence your tax situation, it may be a good move to convert your traditional IRA to a Roth IRA, or your 401(k) into a Roth 401(k). As mentioned in the last chapter, these are tax-exempt investments as opposed to tax-deferred. What it means is, you pay income taxes on your account now, and when you reach retirement age, the distributions are tax-free. If it's a Roth IRA, there will be no RMDs whatsoever. If it's a Roth 401(k), there will be RMDs when you turn seventy-two, but they will be tax-free.

This may or may not be the right move depending on your income, employer, and age. Generally speaking, it's more worthwhile the younger you are because then the retirement fund has time to appreciate before distributions.

2. Make Qualified Charitable Distributions (QCDs)

As you may know, many charitable contributions can reduce your taxable income. You may not know that you can use your tax-deferred retirement account to make charitable contributions, called Qualified Charitable Distributions (QCDs).

You can donate to certain charitable organizations directly from your IRA, including many churches, nonprofit organizations, educational organizations, and other 501(c)3 organizations. This donation can take care of some or all of your RMDs for a year (QCDs are capped at $100,000 per person, across all tax-deferred accounts).

It's tougher, and less beneficial, to take the RMD, donate most of it to a charitable organization, and then write it off. There are certain limitations on deducting charitable donations and donating to charity without using a QCD does not lower your MAGI, which affects Medicare premiums among other things.

So you could withdraw your RMD and donate some of it to the charitable organization of your choice. Or you could make a QCD, which ensures that all the money in your RMD goes to the cause you want. This can be especially helpful if you have other income sources, like rental income or capital gains coming in from investments. Regardless, a QCD is one of the few ways to ensure that the IRS gets 0 percent of the RMD, by diverting your retirement savings to a charity.

3. Have a Plan for Your RMDs (and Potential Penalties)

Regardless of the steps you take to mitigate taxes on your RMDs, you need to have a plan for them. Ignorance is not a tenable legal defense, especially where taxes are concerned. If you have a tax-deferred Retirement Savings Account (RSA) and reach age seventy-two, they'll come.

If you miss an RMD, it's not the end of the world. Consider Bob's case. His penalty if he didn't withdraw that $36,496.35 would be $18,248.18, leaving him with $981,751.82. So his account would have to grow by about 2 percent to accommodate that loss. Now, the penalty would grow as he aged and his factor number decreased, thus increasing the RMD and the penalty. If Bob made it to the ripe old age of 115 and still had $1,000,000, for example, his factor number would be 2.9 and his RMD would be about $344,827, with a penalty of about $172,414. Thus, missing RMDs is never a good long-term solution.

Take the time to review your retirement situation, and plan accordingly. In Strategies 6 and 15, we'll give you more information to help you decide whether Roth conversions and QCDs are the right move for you.

Chapter Summary

The house always wins, and the IRS always finds a way to tax your income. Or at least, virtually always. This is why Congress established Required Minimum Distributions (RMDs) on tax-deferred Retirement Savings Accounts. They're a mandatory yearly withdrawal, calculated by your balance and your age once you turn seventy-two. Plus, they count toward your total taxable income for the year.

RMDs can affect your Social Security and Medicare situation. They also carry a heavy penalty if you miss them. So make sure you have a plan and a strategy for them. Some people decide to donate some or all of their RMDs to a charity of their choice in a Qualified Charitable Distribution (QCD). Others convert their retirement account into a Roth IRA or Roth 401(k) to avoid RMDs or taxes on RMDs respectively.

Regardless, it's important to have a plan. If you have a tax-deferred retirement plan, for almost everyone, RMDs will come the year after you turn seventy-two.

Chapter Takeaways:

✓ To ensure people can't dodge taxes indefinitely with tax-deferred retirement plans, the IRS instituted RMDs.

✓ These distributions count toward your total taxable income each year.

✓ There are a couple of methods to reduce (or eliminate) RMDs or the taxes on them, but they require forethought. These include QCDs and Roth conversions.

Building Block #4:
Getting Intentional with *Where* You Pay Taxes

T his chapter mostly has to do with specific state tax rules. These may not seem like they apply to you at the moment because it shouldn't matter what the next state over does for taxes, but they become extremely important in retirement planning. Because taxes can vary so much from state to state, people often encounter unexpected taxes when they move for their retirement (whether the move is planned or unexpected).

Let's continue the saga of Bob, the retiree. As we mentioned earlier, Bob worked hard for his entire career and saved money in a 401(k). By the end of his career, he had contributed $500,000 to the account. It also grew on its own to $1,000,000.

In Building Block #2, we helped Bob understand the difference between tax-deferred and tax-free retirement accounts. Because his 401(k) is tax-deferred, he enjoyed sizable tax deductions on his contributions, but now that he's retiring, he will need to pay money on his distributions.

He also can't simply refuse to take money out during his retirement. After he turns seventy-two, Required Minimum Distributions

(RMDs) will kick in, essentially forcing him to withdraw a portion of his funds, which will then be taxed. Bob understands all of this, and he has planned accordingly.

Now, the day has come when Bob is ready to retire! His workplace throws him a party, his boss presents him with a gold watch, and he goes on his merry way.

Bob knows that he doesn't want to stay in his current state of residence. He wants to soak up the sun, relax on the beach, and maybe take up dune buggy racing. So he moves to California.

Thanks to our work in the previous chapters, Bob is prepared for federal income tax for his retirement. He has a plan for his RMDs. But one thing he's failed to consider is how changing states might affect his tax situation.

State Taxes Apply Too

The focus of this book has been on federal taxes. They're the taxes that apply to all of us. We talk about them in this book because we all have them in common, and they tend to be much larger than state income taxes. If we went through the ins and outs of each state, this book would get extremely long … and most of it wouldn't really apply to you.

For the purpose of not getting killed on taxes, you need to understand the federal rules and those of your current state. However, few people also think about the states they might move to. This move could come from their job or from retirement.

Where you retire has a huge impact on how far your hard-earned savings will go. That's why it's important to gain an understanding of the rules for each location. It could save you thousands of dollars during the time in your life when you should be least concerned about finances. So how do we prepare for moving states?

Each state has its own rules. For example, some states have a retail sales tax, and others don't. Some have a relatively high property tax level, and others have it lower. Also, certain states have car tabs, essentially a tax for vehicle ownership, that can vary depending on the sort of vehicle you own.

Additionally, some states (New Jersey and Oregon) don't let motorists pump their own gas if there's a station attendee present. That doesn't have much to do with taxes, but it illustrates how frequently small, unexpected facets of life can vary from state to state. The same certainly applies to tax obligations.

An Example: Bob's Story

We've established that planning for specific destination states should be part of your overall tax strategy. Let's look at Bob's story to drive the point home. As mentioned before, Bob wants to move to California when he retires, mostly for the warm weather and beaches … and maybe for the extreme motorsports.

How will moving to California during his retirement affect his tax situation?

1. California is One of the Highest-Taxed States in the Country

To start, Bob has to prepare for higher taxes, period. California has a relatively high sales tax on most items. This varies from county to county, but the minimum is 7.25 percent. Though the tax is technically imposed on the retailer, not the consumer, the retailer can and will charge the consumer for the taxes of a sale in most cases.

On top of this, there is a use tax levied on purchasers that applies to most sales. This tax applies to anyone storing, using, or consuming tangible personal property … so pretty much everything money can buy. If Bob's coming from say, Oregon, where there is no sales tax, then he may be blindsided by an additional 7.25 percent to 11 percent tax on all his purchases.

2. California (Along with Forty Other States) Levies Additional Income Taxes on Top of Federal Income Tax

Some states, nine to be exact, have no income tax, but most do. Some states have a flat rate that they charge on all income, some tax only capital gains, and others have full income tax brackets, similar in concept to the federal brackets. California is one of the states with its own income tax brackets, ranging from 1 percent to a whopping 13.3 percent as of the 2022 tax year. Remember, this is in addition to federal income tax. Bob will have to examine the bracket he will end up in and plan accordingly for any sources of income for his retirement.

3. California Fully Taxes Income on Retirement Accounts

Remember, Bob has a 401(k), which means that his distributions will count toward his taxable income. They will count not only toward federal income tax but also toward California's income tax. Certain states make retirement distributions and pensions exempt from state income tax, but not the Golden State. So Bob needs to realize that his 401(k) distributions will be getting taxed at the state and federal level.

At the end of the day, Bob could end up paying thousands of dollars more in taxes than he was expecting, just by merit of moving across state lines. He needs to take this into account when he plans for his retirement. If he's still California dreaming, then he needs a plan for the high taxes. If this knowledge bursts his bubble, he may need to start looking for somewhere else to plant his rocking chair.

This is just one example. The idiosyncrasies of each state can vary dramatically, but taking the time to prepare will help tremendously.

How to Prepare for Your "Where"

There are a few proactive steps everyone can take now ahead of their retirement. No, you don't have to become an expert on the ins and outs of every state in the union. However, you do need to understand the rules of your current location and your prospective destinations.

Yes, we are very focused on taxes in this book, but even with that focus, we will be the first to tell you that taxes are not the only (or necessarily even best) reason to make a decision. One way to think about this is that taxes are an important passenger on the bus of your life decisions, but never the driver. When deciding where to live, start with prioritizing family, friends, and hobbies, but don't forget to research the taxes so you know what you are getting into.

1. Study Your State's Tax Rules

Few people have taken the time to really understand their own state's rules. Some know them from experience and assume that taxes are just the same in other states. Others aren't really sure about their state's specific rules.

Take the time to research your state's tax landscape. Read directly from your state's Department of Revenue, as well as secondhand sources. Understand what makes your state unique. You might find that staying put when you retire is the best move financially. At any rate, you'll have something to compare with your destinations.

Also, we understand that some people *don't plan to move* when they retire. In this case, it's doubly important for them to understand the rules of their home state. If you do plan to move, however, you should still research your home state. That way, you're covered if the move doesn't work out, or if you have to move back for any reason.

2. Plan Your Retirement Destination(s)

You may not be certain where you'll move when you retire, but you probably have a general idea. You need to decide the kind of lifestyle you want, how close you want to live to your kids and extended family, the weather … and a million other factors.

We recommend making a list of the top two to five destinations you have in mind so that you don't get overwhelmed with research. Then, answer the following questions for them:

- What rules does the state have for property tax, income tax, and sales tax?
- How does the state treat IRA and other retirement plan distributions?
- Does the destination state tax Social Security income? Some do, and some don't.
- Are there any special taxes or uncommon rules to be aware of?

Here's something else to think about: Some retirees go away to a different state for a time, and then decide they want to move back to be closer to their kids and grandkids. There's nothing wrong with that, as long as they understand how their tax situation will be affected and plan accordingly. Others move to one state for a while, and then move to a third state. At the end of the day, it's all about research and preparation.

3. Lend Your Knowledge to Your Children, Friends, and Parents

Lastly, this knowledge shouldn't just stay with you. If you have parents close to retirement age, have a conversation with them. This sets them up for success in their own retirement.

Or maybe your children or friends plan to move. Make sure they realize that their tax situation could change. We've encountered too many stories of people being hit with nasty surprises come tax season because they moved to a new state and didn't read the fine print. So spread the word!

Now that Bob understands the tax rules in California, he's ready to settle down by the beach. He can plan his yearly distributions and monthly budget accordingly and have the peace of mind he's worked so hard for. That can be your story too, as long as you prepare for it.

Chapter Summary

Retirement ought to be the most stress-free, simple time in a person's life. However, many people encounter tax surprises because they move to a new location during retirement.

These surprises can be avoided through planning and preparation. Everyone should understand the tax rules of their home state, as well as the top two to five destinations they might want to move to.

Plus, when someone has a good understanding of certain states, they can lend that knowledge to their friends and family.

Chapter Takeaways:

✓ There are major differences between states regarding tax rules.

✓ Not everyone considers how moving during their retirement will affect their tax situation.

✓ Take the time to plan your top destinations, study them, and compare them to your current state.

Building Block #5:

Having a System to Capture Every Benefit You're Entitled To

mid the sea of complexity in our tax code, there are several limitations on how much of a good (or bad) thing a taxpayer can use in a single year to help lower their overall tax obligations. Good things include tax credits and refundable tax credits. "Bad" things include losses that can be written off.

The key is to keep track of every benefit you're entitled to so that you can maximize each tax season. This is an important building block for an effective tax strategy, but remember, it's not the only one. Some people assume that the goal is to get the biggest possible refund each year. We disagree, since your "refund" was your money all along. The IRS just held onto it for you, as a sort of interest-free loan. The goal should instead be to plan so the IRS keeps as little of your hard-earned money as possible over your lifetime, all while holding on to your own money the whole time.

You can also carry forward taxable losses from one year into the next year, to further reduce your taxable income for that year. Furthermore, there are certain areas that get overlooked that could further boost your benefits.

So how can you make sure you take advantage of every benefit you can? It ultimately comes down to developing a system.

Document Everything

Start keeping track of all the tax benefits you can get. To this end, many taxpayers use a tax organizer template that they can reuse every year. This is a checklist, or a set of questions about your tax status. You go through and answer every item, and for certain answers, you get a deduction.

This is a great system for keeping track of tax-related changes that happen in your life during the year. It could be gaining or losing a dependent, going back to school, or buying a home. It could also be things we don't always think about. For example, if you worked at home during the pandemic or afterward, you may be entitled to a deduction for your utilities, internet, cell phone, or maybe even a home office since you used it for work.

You can create a tax organizer yourself or find a template online. If you use a CPA, they most likely have one they use to fill out your 1040 anyway. However, you shouldn't wait until tax season to start documenting your benefits.

Some people we work with start treating this like a game or a puzzle. Their objective is to get as many benefits and deductions as possible. That's far better than a mindset of stress or anxiety when it comes to taxes, so if that works for you, try it. Don't just rely on a preparer or preparation software.

This goes back to the fact that the software isn't perfect. It will miss benefits that you're entitled to. It doesn't always ask every question, or you may not understand the questions it asks you (tax rules are written by politicians, not accountants ... although having accountants write the rules might not make them easier to understand). Sometimes tax rules change and the software doesn't update. Other times, as we alluded to back in Myth #4, it applies rules that aren't valid anymore.

In the worst case, preparation software can even give you benefits you're not entitled to ... which, again, leads to nasty surprises during tax season or in the event of an audit. Speaking of worst cases ...

Two Worst-Case Scenarios

You should also document things like the buying and selling of assets that will count toward capital gains and losses. You need to be able to provide evidence for basis (how much you originally paid) in stock sales, and also use that as proof if you need to.

Imagine you begin investing in a mutual fund. Sometimes, you don't just pay for shares, but you also pay a commission. In this case, your basis is the purchase price after commissions, not to mention any other expenses associated with the purchase or sale.

Few people track this really well. One taxpayer that Steven worked with didn't understand what basis was. Instead of taking the time to understand what it meant, he reported the basis on his investments as $0, even though his investment obviously had a cost of above $0 when he bought them. So, in this case, the entire amount the investment was sold for would count as a gain, even if the investment lost money. That "gain" then counted toward his total taxable income and was liable for capital gains tax.

On a related note, there was another couple Steven worked with who made nondeductible IRA contributions throughout the year. ("Nondeductible?" Don't worry, we'll cover this later on.) You can do that in both traditional and Roth IRAs. All Roth IRA contributions are nondeductible, and for traditional IRAs, some contributions aren't eligible for deductions. In this case, the couple simply chose not to get a deduction for their contribution to their traditional IRA so that it would grow tax-free.

They assumed that they didn't need to report anything about the contribution. After all, the contribution would be taxed as part of their income/gains for that year.

However, when you can't prove you paid taxes on a portion of your income that went into an IRA, what do you think the IRS is going to do when you withdraw that money? If you guessed "tax you again," then give yourself a point, and get out your checkbook. This couple ended up paying taxes on the same income twice due to a lack of tracking and reporting.

Long story short: we need to develop a system that tracks everything coming in and going out, in addition to the requisite forms associated with our income and investments.

First, document all of your income. This might be pay stubs you file away, business income, rental income, capital gains, you name it. Keep track of it and report all of it.

Next, document every expenditure that can be written off as a deduction. This includes the obvious like business expenses and tuition, but also the less obvious like miles driven for business or phone bills for work.

After this, document all of your investments, even if they aren't deductions themselves. This way, you won't get taxed twice like the aforementioned couple.

Finally, keep everything in one place. If it's a tax spreadsheet on your computer, make sure it's backed up. Plus, file every paper tax form you get in the same place.

Oft-Overlooked Areas

In our experience, there are a few areas that get overlooked when it comes to documentation that could help (or hurt):

1. Tax Loss Carryover

There are limits to how much of a loss you can take on your tax return in a single year. These losses aren't lost forever; they get carried forward to future years *if* you remember to report them. They essentially reduce your taxable income in future years, up to $3,000 a year after offsetting any gains during the year. All it takes is a bit of planning and, again, documentation.

So say you invest $100,000 into a fund, and it's your only investment. In the first year, it loses $9,000 to be worth $91,000. This will give you a net capital loss of $9,000 if you sell it at a loss. You can then use that loss to write off $3,000 in income in the current year and each year for the following two years. But only if you are keeping track and reporting the losses.

First, you need to track the tax basis, which we covered above. In this case, it's $100,000. Then, you need to determine your net capital gains from all your investments. For example, if you had other investments besides the $100,000 that appreciated enough, it could nullify the loss if you also sold those investments. You have to do the math on all your investments to see.

If the total is negative, then those losses can be carried over. The amount you can write off is $3,000 a year, or $1,500 if you're married filing separately. You can continue to carry that loss over to future years until it's gone.

The only exception is if you buy back the investment within thirty days of selling it at a loss. This becomes subject to "wash sale" rules and adds to the complexity.

To take advantage of this rule, you fill out Form 8949 and Schedule D of your 1040 (capital gains and losses) like normal. Then, you can use the Capital Loss Carryover Worksheet in the instructions of Schedule D. Finally, enter it on line 14 of your Schedule D.

2. Form 8606

Form 8606 comes into play for nondeductible IRA contributions. Remember the couple from earlier who failed to track and report these contributions and ended up getting taxed twice? Completing this form prevents that situation. Form 8606 is made to keep track of the tax basis of assets, whether they're pretax or after-tax. Pretax is like the tax-deferred money in a traditional IRA or 401(k) that we discussed in Building Block #2. After-tax is tax-free when you distribute it ... if you can prove it.

If you convert funds to a Roth IRA or contribute to a traditional IRA that you don't (or can't) claim a deduction for, then you need to fill out

Form 8606 and report it. This essentially tells the IRS that they're taxing you for those contributions as part of your regular income.

Why wouldn't someone just take the tax deduction the moment they invest? If you don't deduct your traditional IRA contributions, then you can more easily convert the dollars to Roth and get the distributions for it tax- and penalty-free. But again, only if you do an airtight job proving it by tracking it through this form.

To sum it up, Form 8606 is your friend if you don't want to tip the IRS. Make sure to check whether you need to fill it out every year, and ask your preparer about it if you use one.

3. Alternative Minimum Tax (AMT)

At the beginning of the chapter, we talked about how there's a limit on how much you can do to lower your tax obligations on a yearly basis. This limit is essentially determined by an Alternative Minimum Tax (AMT). This set of rules was devised to prevent certain taxpayers from getting so many tax breaks that they owe nothing.

The AMT essentially works by adding certain items that you wrote off back into your Adjusted Gross Income (AGI) so that you have taxable income again. It only kicks in if you make a certain amount and have certain types of income or transactions, however. In 2022, it's about $76,000 for single and married filing separately, and about $118,000 for married filing jointly. The rules switch again for those with a single income of about $523,000 or a joint income of about $1,080,000. The first amount ($76,000 and $118,000) is no longer exempt from the overall calculation.

If you think you might be liable for an AMT, you can figure it out using IRS Form 6251.[4] It takes information about certain deductions, investments, and income for you to get your answer. It's something

---

4   U.S. Department of the Treasury, Internal Revenue Service, Form 6251, (Washington, DC: 2021), https://www.irs.gov/pub/irs-pdf/f6251.pdf.

Steven does for clients whose income falls in a certain range to make sure they don't end up in hot water for taking too many deductions.

The bottom line? Document and track everything, even if you aren't sure of the importance of it at the moment. You need to know all the money you have coming in and going out if you want to minimize your taxes. Develop a spreadsheet and keep a file. Create or borrow a tax organizer for yearly use. Check every year whether you have net capital gains or losses, or whether you can carry the losses from a previous year over. Determine if you need to fill out Form 8606, or whether you might owe AMT.

If you do all these things, you'll maximize your benefits while mitigating your liabilities (and penalties). You'll have a system.

Putting the Building Blocks Together

Maximizing your benefits is the final building block for an effective tax strategy. We hope you see the importance of documentation and even gamifying the experience to take away the pressure or anxiety.

Let's do a quick review of the previous building blocks, so we can use them in our tax strategy:

- Building Block #1 was about managing your income tax and capital gains brackets. Not everyone realizes that they have separate brackets, and that capital gains aren't in a silo, but count toward your total taxable income. Here, we also talked about *effective* tax rate, the ultimate number when it comes to your yearly filing.
- After this, we talked about tax-deferred and tax-free investment opportunities and the differences between them. We concluded that Roth IRAs are one of the best investment strategies because they grow and get distributed tax-free. They also have a relatively flexible rule set for withdrawals before you reach retirement age, which can help for major unexpected expenses.

- Then, we discussed Required Minimum Distributions (RMDs), essentially a way for the IRS to make sure your tax-deferred retirement accounts eventually get taxed. When you turn seventy-two, you generally need to begin withdrawing a portion of your account. You can avoid RMDs entirely by converting to a Roth IRA, and you can avoid taxes on them by converting to a Roth 401(k) if you're eligible. Additionally, Qualified Charitable Distributions reduce the taxable income from RMDs, but they go to a charitable organization instead of your bank account.
- Just before this chapter, we talked about how state laws affect taxes and retirement planning. Not everyone thinks through how moving during retirement (or for a job, etc.) will affect their tax situation. We encouraged you to list out the other places you might live and gain an understanding of their tax rules.
- Finally, we covered documentation, tax benefits, and often-overlooked deductions and liabilities.

When you understand all of these factors, and use them in your overall tax strategy, you'll be leagues ahead of the average taxpayer. They're the building blocks we'll play with during Part 3: Tax Strategies to Avoid Getting Killed on Taxes. This is why we gave a high-level overview of them. Now, we'll dive more in-depth on nearly every principle that was mentioned in this part and discuss how they can interact to lower your overall tax obligations.

Chapter Summary

Many taxpayers miss out on tax benefits and deductions because they simply don't know about them. They need to begin tracking every possible deduction and benefit they're entitled to because the IRS certainly won't. This can involve building a master tax document on the computer (that gets backed up), in addition to a secure paper filing system and a yearly tax organizer.

We also discussed a few relatively obscure tax rules and principles that can benefit you … or save you from a penalty. This included net capital gains loss carryover, Form 8606 for tax-free assets (think money in Roth IRAs or nondeducted contributions to other retirement plans), and Alternative Minimum Tax (AMT), the ultimate limitation on how many deductions that people over a certain gross income can get away with.

We also summed up the contents of Part 2: Taxes 101: Building Blocks for Effective Tax Strategy so we can build on them during the next section.

Chapter Takeaways:

✓ It's crucial to track and document your income, investments, benefits, and deductions.

✓ If you don't, you could either get penalized or simply miss out on paying less in taxes over your lifetime.

✓ There are a few lesser known rules that can significantly affect your tax situation that you should check for each year. These include loss carryovers, 8606 reporting, and AMT.

Part 3:

Tax Strategies to Avoid Getting Killed on Taxes

Now we have the foundation and the basic building blocks, we can start putting them together. This section uses the principles we've covered so far and goes into greater depth. It will be the final section of the book.

In our time working with countless people to take control of their taxes (and finances in general), we've come across common strategies that help people lower their taxes, save more, and end up with greater financial freedom.

By combining the building blocks with these strategies, not only will you avoid getting killed on taxes but you'll also find yourself with more disposable income during the year.

We'll break down these strategies into the following twenty chapters:

- ➤ Review Safe Harbor Requirements for Federal and State Taxes to Avoid Underpayment Penalties
- ➤ Max Out Tax-Advantaged Retirement Accounts While Working
- ➤ Tax-Aware Investment: Optimize Investment Accounts for Tax Efficiency
- ➤ Make the Right IRA Contributions
- ➤ Utilize All Available Retirement Plan Options
- ➤ Review Roth IRA Conversion Possibilities
- ➤ Evaluate Low-Cost Variable Annuity Contributions
- ➤ Consider Funding a Health Savings Account

➢ Strategically Harvest Capital Gains

➢ Strategically Harvest Tax Losses

➢ Review Income Shifting Strategies for Tax Bracket Smoothing/ Leveraging and More

➢ Minimize Net Investment Income Tax Obligations

➢ Consider Bunching Strategies for Itemized Deductions

➢ Manage Medicare (IRMAA) Brackets

➢ Evaluate Possible Qualified Charitable Distributions, or QCDs

➢ Gifting Strategies to Reduce Overall Tax Obligations

➢ Using Charitable Remainder Trusts to Reduce Tax Obligations

➢ Strategically Using 529 Plans to Save for Education While Minimizing Taxes

➢ Using the S Election to Save Employment Taxes

➢ Using the Augusta Rule to Generate Truly Tax-Free Income

Strategy #1:

Review Safe Harbor Requirements for Federal and State Taxes to Avoid Underpayment Penalties

P aul and Angela Corbin were a couple P. J. worked with, who had estimated tax payments throughout the year. They were in a situation where they had dozens of income sources, making accounting for their income (and estimating their tax payments) difficult.

If you don't pay enough in estimated taxes, you become subject to an underpayment penalty. This penalty varies depending on your income and the state in which you reside. As we mentioned in Building Block #4, different states have different rules when it comes to taxes. Regardless, any avoidable penalty stings. Not to mention, it adds stress to the whole idea of taxes for the next year.

Angela and Paul ended up paying $3,100 in federal penalties in 2018, and an extra $60 from their state of Pennsylvania. This was due to under-payment on their estimated taxes. They weren't sure how much they were going to make, so they neglected to pay the estimated payments.

As you can imagine, the subject of taxes was stressful for them due to their huge number of income sources. This led to them failing to get all of their tax documentation for 2019 turned in until 2020, leading to more penalties ($2,800, to be exact).

That's when we decided to set them up on a safe harbor schedule for tax year 2020.

What Are Safe Harbor Rules?

Safe harbor rules are provisions in the federal (and some states') tax code that help people avoid penalties on the underpayment of taxes. They also help people who are required to make *estimated tax payments* throughout the year, like Angela and Paul, who own multiple businesses.

When you plan for safe harbor rules in your current year and future year, and monitor it carefully, you can potentially save thousands of dollars in penalties. How does it work?

You have to pay 100 percent of last year's tax liability, or 90 percent of the current year's liability, whichever is less, to avoid a penalty on your taxes for the current year. So, if your total liability was $3,000 last year, and $4,000 this year, you'd have to make $3,000 (100 percent of last year's liability) worth of payments before year's end to "safe harbor" your income.

However, if your liability was $3,000 for both years, then you'd need to put in $2,700 (90 percent of last year's liability) for safe harbor rules to take effect. It takes the lower number into account. Since you don't know for sure what your liability will be for the current year until it ends, it's generally a safe bet to go off the previous year's income and liability.

Note: The rule changes slightly when your Adjusted Gross Income (AGI) is greater than $150,000 ($75,000 for filing separately). In this case, you need to pay the lower of these two:

- 110% of last year's liability
- 90% of this year's liability

Depending on your income situation, either one of those could be the lower number. It's rare though when 90 percent of this year's liability exceeds 110 percent of last year's because that would represent a significant increase in income.

A good way to be covered in any case is to take your total tax liability for one year, multiply it by 0.25 (or 0.275 for the higher AGI), and make that your payment in April, June, September, and January. Then, rinse and repeat for the following year.

It's also important not to overpay if it can be avoided. Some people want to make sure their income is safe harbored, so they might make a huge estimated tax payment. By the end of the year, their payments may far exceed 100 percent of last year's liability. Now, if they do end up truly overpaying, they'll get a refund of the difference.

But we already covered in Myth #3 that getting a big tax refund shouldn't be our goal. Any money in your refund is essentially an interest-free loan to the IRS. *It was always your money!* Instead, you want to do that math and hit that 100 percent or 110 percent mark without too much overpayment.

P. J.'s team explained all of this to Angela and Paul.

What Happened to Angela and Paul?

First, P. J.'s team got all their documents in and organized. They needed to know all their income sources and be able to prove them. This was complicated because Angela and Paul had income from thirty-seven K-1s (a document for S corps and/or income from business partners). These sources of income were spread out through 15 states and two countries. Not to mention, the team also had to sort through brokerage statements, savings accounts, and a good old W-2s.

By the time they had everything sorted out, P. J.'s team knew the couple's total income from 2019 and had a good estimate of what they'd make in 2020. But either way, all they had to do was schedule payments adding up to 100 percent of their obligations for the previous year. This way, even if they made more in 2020, they'd still be penalty-free. Again, the total in estimated tax payments has to be either 100 percent or 110 percent of your previous year's income depending on whether your AGI was over or under $150,000 respectively.

Once Paul and Angela set that schedule and followed it, they were able to meet safe harbor requirements for this year. This meant that no matter what, they wouldn't have to pay any penalties for the 2020 tax year—and they didn't. This ultimately saved them about $3,000 in penalties.

No, You Can't True-up Your Withholdings at the End

Cody and Eleanor Thompson are another couple P. J. worked with. Their story shows a common misunderstanding of safe harbor rules. In 2020, Cody thought he could true-up his annual withholding in December with a year-end quarterly payment. For those unfamiliar, this is a strategy used in investing negotiations when you have an estimate of a price when you buy, and it ends up being different after you close. That year, Cody's estimate of his liabilities was much lower than the true value—$60,000 lower to be precise.

So Cody's thought was he could make a big quarterly payment at the end to take care of his liability for 2020. Unfortunately, it doesn't quite work that way. When all was said and done, they had an underpayment of $60,000 and were liable for taxes and penalties.

Thankfully, the Thompsons didn't have to pay a penalty because they made significantly more money in 2020. This is due to another safe harbor rule: If 90 percent of your current year's tax is higher than 110 percent of last year's tax, you're safe. The rule essentially comes into play when you own a business and its income increases by a huge amount one year. Yet, this rule probably wouldn't apply to Cody and Eleanor in 2021.

P. J.'s team fixed it by making a better payment schedule for them. We adjusted Cody's withholding in 2021 to mitigate any additional tax payments at year-end. This is because the IRS views withholding tax annually but estimated tax payments quarterly. A good withholding strategy should consider both factors. Now, they're projected to get a small refund with zero penalties.

What Do These Rules Mean for You?

Given these examples, there are a few ways you should respond to make sure your income is always safe harbored.

First, don't rely on any automatic safe harbor rule. The year 2020 showed us that you simply never know whether your income will be the same from year to year, significantly higher, or significantly lower. The automatic rule only applies when it's significantly higher. Still, you can be protected by setting a schedule … and you won't lose anything if your income ends up being higher anyway.

If you're on estimated tax payments, make a schedule to fulfill 100 percent of last year's taxes (or 110 percent if your AGI was over $150,000). The worst-case scenario here is you end up paying slightly too much due to having less income this year. If that happens, you get a small refund. You can then roll that refund directly into the next year's estimated tax payments, if you want.

P. J.'s office helped Samantha Vo of Pennsylvania with this. Instead of an underpayment, she ended her year with an *overpayment* of $600 toward her Pennsylvania taxes in 2020. At the same time, they knew her PA tax liability was $400 total for that year. If she met 100 percent of that, then her income for 2021 would be safe harbored. So they recommended she apply $400 of that $600 overpayment to her 2021 estimated account, securing safe harbor for 2021.

Second, review your state's rules. Angela, Paul, and Samantha are in PA, which has additional rules and penalties. Likewise, you need to understand how your state affects safe harbor rules. For example, some states have income tax and some don't. Other states have unique tax rules. So take the time to learn about your situation.

Third, understand that you don't have to exclusively withhold your *income* for these estimates. Almost everyone has multiple streams of income, all of which can influence estimated tax payments. For instance, you can withhold taxes from your Social Security payments. You get to decide where the money comes from for your estimated payments, so make sure every stream pays its fair share. It could be important to review this with a professional, which could save you money.

Here's an example: Glenn and Alan Holmes were on a safe harbor schedule set by P. J.'s office. They had outside bank savings accounts (which included Certificates of Deposit, or CDs), creating multiple cash flows. Glenn mentioned that they weren't receiving a significant amount of interest on their investments since interest rates were decreasing. So P. J.'s team reviewed their quarterly safe harbor payments and determined they didn't need to pay an extra estimated tax payment. In other words, they kept the money in their accounts instead of overpaying and receiving a refund later. This way, their money kept working for them instead of getting loaned to the IRS, interest free.

To sum it up, safe harbor rules can protect you from penalties, especially if you own a business and your income increases year over year. It's up to you, however, to create a schedule and make timely payments that add up to one of the minimum liabilities.

Chapter Summary

Safe harbor rules are a method by which taxpayers can avoid penalties on underpayments. They come into play most often when the taxpayer has income besides their W-2 employment and must make estimated tax payments on a quarterly basis.

For people under $150,000 Adjusted Gross Income (AGI), they should pay in 100 percent of their previous year's tax liability to avoid penalties, regardless of their income this year. For people with income over the threshold, it's 110 percent of their previous year's tax liability.

Any overpayments will come back as a refund. In that case, the taxpayer could choose to roll that money into their estimated payments for the next year.

Chapter Takeaways:

✓ If you are required to make estimated tax payments, they have to total above a certain threshold, based on your previous year's and current year's tax liabilities, or you're underpaying.

✓ Underpayment can cause some hefty penalties, and they usually come unexpectedly.

✓ Make sure your estimated payments are scheduled and add up to 100% of your previous year's liability, or 110% if your AGI was over $150,000. The IRS has a free tool, known as the Tax Withholding Estimator, to help with this. You can find a direct link to the Tax Withholding Estimator on DontGetKilledOnTaxes.com.

✓ To safe harbor your taxes, pay 100% of last year's tax or 90% of the current year, whichever is less. If you earn over $150,000, pay 110% of the previous year's tax or 90% of the current year, whichever is less.

Strategy #2:

Max Out Tax-Advantaged Retirement Accounts While Working

The next strategy involves investing the maximum amount in tax-advantaged retirement accounts during your working years. What is a tax-advantaged account? Any tax-deferred or tax-exempt account, or one that offers a tax benefit in general. If it's at all possible, it will benefit you greatly to contribute the maximum amount to one of these accounts—or multiple.

There are two main paths that you can take here, depending on which kind of account you prioritize. It all comes down to whether you will benefit from paying taxes on your investments now, or later on when you retire. We covered the difference between tax-deferred and tax-exempt accounts back in Building Block #2 if you need a refresher.

Though many people take a hybrid approach, you still have to prioritize one kind of account at the end of the day. Even if you have just $1 to invest in retirement, which account do you put it in to get the best results? The following two strategies explain the accounts you can choose and the circumstances that would make you choose them.

1: Tax-Deferred Investments

The first path is to prioritize tax-deferred investments. These include retirement plans like the typical workplace 401(k) or 403(b), and Individual Retirement Accounts (IRAs). If the taxpayer has a retirement plan, they can also decide to make direct contributions from their salary as elective-deferral contributions. Sometimes these are called salary-reduction contributions as well.

Even though elective-deferral contributions have cases where they're after-tax, if a person follows a tax-deferred strategy, they will likely decide to make them pretax. Elective-deferral contributions and contributions to traditional IRAs reduce your current income tax by reducing your total taxable income.

The money that you put into a tax-deferred account doesn't count toward your overall tax obligations for that year, which saves you money in the short term. This money could then be invested into other streams of income.

When Should Someone Take the Tax-Deferred Path?

There are two primary situations where it's best to prioritize deferring your taxes. They both have to do with the fact that you pay taxes later, instead of now.

The first situation comes when you're in a high tax bracket now, but plan to be in a lower tax bracket after you retire. This is the classic retirement investment strategy. Take, for instance, the story of Nick and Olivia Jameson, clients of P. J.'s office.

Nick and Olivia are in a high income tax bracket. (Note: we covered tax brackets for income and capital gains back in Building Block #1.) This means their effective tax rate would be high unless they do something about it. So they have decided to max out their individual 401(k)s through their respective workplaces on a yearly basis.

They invest $26,000 each into these tax-deferred accounts for a total of $52,000 a year. Lowering their total taxable income by $52,000 each year makes a tremendous difference. Before these adjustments, they were landing in the 32 percent tax bracket. Since they're deferring taxes on a large chunk of their income, they're now in the 24 percent bracket. After doing the math, P. J.'s team determined that Nick and Olivia are able to save up to $16,000 on taxes each year.

This leads us to the second reason to pursue this strategy: Investments tend to appreciate and compound over time. Because Nick and Olivia are deferring taxes, they are able to invest more each year into their 401(k)s than they would with, say, a Roth 401(k) or Roth IRA. Plus, the $16,000 they save on taxes each year? They could invest that money wherever they like, further snowballing the growth.

Ideally, Nick and Olivia will continue this strategy, let their savings grow, and retire comfortably. Once retired, they'll take distributions from these funds as income, and it will be taxed then. If the taxpayer plans correctly, they'll be in higher tax brackets during their career (but push themselves lower with tax-deferred investments), and then be in lower brackets when they retire.

However, as we covered in Myth #6 and Building Block #3 (Required Minimum Distributions), this isn't always the case. In fact, if a taxpayer has built a sizable retirement account with pretax investments, they could reasonably expect to remain in the same bracket when they retire, or even go up. This effect compounds too since Nick and Olivia were pushing themselves down a tax bracket their whole career when their "true" bracket was higher.

These considerations could lead someone to take the second main path.

2: Tax-Exempt Investments

The second path involves emphasizing tax-free or tax-exempt investments. These mostly consist of Roth 401(k)s and Roth IRAs. Additionally, some investments can be made on an after-tax basis. In other words, you decide not to defer taxes on them, and instead pay them as part of your regular income tax that year. This often requires meticulous accounting and reporting since you need to prove to the IRS that you already paid taxes on your investments. We covered scenarios like these in Building Block #5.

When you invest into these accounts, you don't gain any kind of tax benefit in the present moment. But when you retire and begin withdrawing money from them, it's entirely tax-free. These distributions don't count toward your taxable income at all, so you may end up in a lower tax bracket when you retire. Unless you have income coming in from other sources, the only taxes you'll pay will be on things like Social Security.

Besides not counting as a deduction in the present, these accounts also have lower maximums. At the time of this writing, you can put $6,000 per year into a Roth account unless you're age fifty or older, in which case you can invest $7,000.

When Should Someone Take the Tax-Exempt Path?

Like the previous strategy, there are a couple of situations where it may be preferable to take the tax-exempt path. It ultimately depends on your age, income, and other investments.

If you're young, you may want to take advantage of the compounding interest of a Roth IRA. The younger you start investing, the more money your account will be worth when you retire. Because the money is distributed tax-free, you get 100 percent of your contributions and the growth back.

Say you have $200,000 in a 401(k) and the exact same amount in a Roth IRA when you retire. If you were to distribute the entire 401(k), you'd typically pay anywhere from $30,000 to $50,000 in taxes on it depending on your tax bracket, capital gains, any other income sources, and deductions such as charitable contributions. However, that $200,000 in the Roth IRA is worth $200,000, and the IRS will never be entitled to any of it.

Plus, as we covered in Building Block #1, there are many situations where you can withdraw your contributions (or even the growth) from your Roth IRA early without penalties, like in the case of a sudden unexpected expense, or the first-time purchase of a home. The penalties or lack thereof depend on your age, the length of time you've had the account, and the way you'll use the money.

An added bonus: The Roth IRA doesn't have RMDs, and the Roth 401(k)'s RMDs are tax-exempt. So some people keep as much money as possible in a Roth IRA while withdrawing the minimum amount they need each year, without worry of any penalty, also called an excise tax. To circumvent RMDs entirely, you may consider converting the Roth 401(k) into a Roth IRA, which we'll cover in more detail in Strategy #6.

So if you're young and in a lower tax bracket, you may want to consider putting as much as possible into a Roth IRA or a Roth 401(k) if your employer offers one. You're qualified to invest in a Roth IRA if your Adjusted Gross Income (AGI) is $144,000 or lower for a single filer. If you're married filing jointly, it's currently $214,000.

Since you're already in a lower bracket, you won't benefit as much from tax-deferred investments as, say, Nick and Olivia.

The other reason you would invest in tax-exempt retirement savings? You're young, you're already maxing out your 401(k) or IRA, and you have extra income to invest. In this case, you may consider putting the money you're saving on taxes into a tax-exempt account as a long-term investment. Again, this becomes more beneficial the younger you are.

Combined and Special Strategies

Whether you decide to prioritize tax-deferred or tax-exempt investments largely comes down to your personal circumstances and preferences. A good advisor won't religiously recommend only one path to all of their clients but will work with each client's situation to determine what's best.

This flexibility is especially important because of all the special rules and requirements that taxes bring—not to mention life's propensity to throw curveballs. Here are a few practical strategies you and your advisor should consider, with real-life examples.

1. Maximize Your Inheritance for Your Retirement

When you inherit money, what should you do with it? This ultimately depends on the tax rules of the money and your overall retirement strategy. Generally speaking, it can be good to put this money into the retirement plan and savings accounts you prioritize so that it can benefit you through tax deductions now, or tax-free distributions later.

For example, take the story of Noah Patrick. He inherited a $500,000 IRA as the designated beneficiary. Due to a new inherited IRA distribution law called the Secure Act 2019, he was required to distribute the entire account in ten years. Noah was also recently married and looking to secure his and his wife's retirement. So we came up with a solution.

P. J.'s team used the mandatory yearly distribution (about $50,000 a year) to max out the couple's 401(k) and an HSA (health savings) account. As of 2022, the yearly limit on two 401(k)s is $41,000, and the limit for the HSA is $7,300, so they can distribute $48,300 in 2022 toward their retirement without that counting toward their total taxable income, a number that will increase over the next ten years as the 401(k) and HSA limits adjust.

2. Leverage Gift Exclusions to Leave Your Legacy

You can exclude the taxes on cash gifts up to $16,000 per donor as of 2022. Some people maximize this exclusion every year to help set up their children and grandchildren for retirement while lowering their taxable income. Here's a story of two taxpayers leveraging this rule.

John Sanders is the son of David and Lina. David and Lina gift John money, up to the annual gifting exclusion limit, every year. That's

$32,000 coming to John while lowering David and Lina's taxable income by the same amount.

In exchange, John uses that money to maximize his 401(k) contributions, which once again is $20,500 each year. So this gives the parents an estate tax benefit by decreasing their taxable estate and allows John to maximize his elected deferral into his 401(k). John also took it a step further: He maxed out a Roth IRA, using an additional $6,000 of that gift each year.

3. Understand Contribution Limits from a Panoramic Perspective

Something not everyone considers is what happens when you go over your contribution limit. A good tax or financial advisor will talk you through the annual contribution limits on your plans. A great one will help you understand them for all qualified plans and help you make an informed decision about where to direct your investments. Consider the story of Susan Miller.

Susan was faithfully contributing to a retirement plan through her employer. One day, her employer was acquired by another company, which dissolved the former company's qualified plan. Taking this in stride, Susan signed up and directed contributions to the qualified plan sponsored by her new employer. The only problem was, she didn't think about the new contribution limits and ended up making an excess contribution to both of her employer-sponsored retirement plans. This incurs a penalty if you can't get the retirement plan company to back out the contributions.

Due to the retirement plan custodian's restrictions, Susan was unable to back out the excess contribution. P. J.'s office advised Susan to roll her orphan 401(k) into an IRA and then take the distributions before the filing deadline. This wasn't ideal, but it allowed her to avoid the excess contribution penalty. As a result, Susan has to open a new rollover IRA and transfer the orphan 401(k) into the rollover to back out her excess contributions. The moral of the story? Stay up to date on contribution limits!

Time to Get Maximizing

We've discussed the main paths people take when it comes to tax-advantaged retirement accounts, in addition to some special situations and provisions. Ultimately, you can't go wrong if you consistently max out contributions to tax-advantaged retirement accounts. However, the accounts you choose will depend on your circumstances. In addition, take note of special rules and contribution limits so that you maximize your benefits, lower your obligations, and avoid unwelcome surprises.

 ## Chapter Summary

Tax-advantaged retirement accounts are any investment that gives you some kind of tax benefit, whether it's for the current year or for your distributions. Ideally, a taxpayer should work to max out their annual contributions to a tax-advantaged account, if not multiple.

Some people prioritize tax-deferred investments, and some prefer tax-exempt investments. However, it is possible to max out both on an annual basis to get the best of both worlds.

Additionally, the tax code has some special rules and provisions regarding retirement accounts to be aware of. Inherited IRAs and 401(k)s need to be distributed within ten years if you're not the spouse or an eligible designated beneficiary. You can combine the annual gift tax exclusion for gifts ($16,000 per person) nicely with the contribution limit of a 401(k) and Roth IRA, $26,500 in total. Lastly, make sure you're aware of the contribution limits of all your investments and potential investments.

Chapter Takeaways:

✓ Ideally, a taxpayer should max out their contributions to all the tax-advantaged retirement accounts available to them.

✓ Sometimes, a taxpayer might prioritize tax-deferred or tax-exempt investments if they have limited funds to work with.

✓ There are a few special rules and strategies to learn and leverage, like contribution limits, gift exclusions, and rules for inheriting IRAs.

Strategy #3:

Tax-Aware Investment:
Optimize Investment Accounts for Tax Efficiency

D o you remember Angela and Paul from Strategy #1? They were a couple who underpaid on their federal taxes for a couple of years in a row, which caused them to pay thousands in federal and state penalties. P. J.'s office created a safe harbor schedule for them to handle their estimated tax payments and ensure they don't get hit with any more penalties.

Around the same time, P. J.'s team also helped them set up an investment portfolio. They wanted to invest their income (plus the money they were about to save on penalties), but they had a specific concern: they wanted to ensure their investing was socially responsible.

What is socially responsible investing? It typically means investing only in causes and companies that you can support. People may have concerns about business practices, social issues, the climate, and more. In this case, they decide to direct their investment funds in a way that aligns with their conscience and top values.

Angela and Paul began working with Carl Hartman, a Financial Wellness LifeCoach™ from P. J.'s team. Carl set to work building a socially responsible portfolio for them. Carl, Angela, and Paul also agreed that they wanted their investments to have an active tax management strategy.

They wanted to reduce their overall tax obligations through their investment portfolio. This usually means writing off losses to offset gains and directing capital into specific funds. When done correctly, this reduces overall tax liability and allows you to keep as much of your gains as possible.

Don't invest without considering the tax implications for everything. After all, if you invest in areas with higher taxes, or fail to balance your losses and gains, you won't make as much money as you could have. Plus, the IRS will be entitled to a greater portion of the gains.

Thankfully, there are rules and strategies to follow that allow us to synergize our investment accounts for tax efficiency.

Three Rules and Strategies for Tax-Aware Investing

Note: A couple of these strategies often require significant investment capital at the start of the process. This means they often work best for high-income earners and affluent/accredited investors. For taxpayers in a lower income bracket, it may be advisable to prioritize tax-exempt retirement accounts and after-tax investments in general.

1. Separately Managed Accounts (SMA)

SMAs are actively traded accounts focused on personalizing the investment experience for the investor. Some funds (i.e., Exchange-Traded Funds, Mutual Funds) take a more hands-off approach, but SMAs are managed directly by an advisor on a regular if not daily basis.

SMAs are a fantastic way to create a custom portfolio tailored for the client's needs, goals, and priorities. In Angela and Paul's case, an SMA ensured their investments only went into areas that fit their criteria for social responsibility.

Carl Hartman, the aforementioned Financial Wellness LifeCoach, spent several years building a relationship with Angela and Paul and managing their portfolio needs. They didn't begin with social responsibility in mind; remember, at the beginning they simply wanted to avoid penalties and right the ship.

As Carl continued working with them, they expressed the desire for socially responsible investment strategies. These often fall under the category of ESG: Environmental, Social, and Governance. At the same time, they wanted to grow the portfolio and keep it tax-efficient.

So Carl came up with a solution: Dimensional Fund Advisors (DFAs) managing their SMA. The DFA's managers knew which funds to invest in based on their ESG and nurtured Angela and Paul's various funds for incremental growth. They also actively harvested the gains and losses in the account and meticulously accounted for everything. This allowed the advisors to harvest the short-term capital losses (STCL) and deduct them against Angela and Paul's other income. By the end of the current year, these losses are projected to save them up to $3,800 in federal income tax.

If you have relatively high income or capital, then a DFA SMA could be a fantastic move for steady growth and regular tax benefits.

2. Wash Sale Rules

Wash sale rules come up whenever you're harvesting capital losses, so it's relevant to break them down now.

Essentially, the rules state that you can't deduct losses from the sale or trade of a security unless the loss was incurred in the ordinary course of your business as a dealer in stock or securities. It prevents investors from selling a losing stock, writing off the losses, and then immediately buying it back.

Here are the specific provisions. A wash sale occurs when you sell or trade stock and securities at a loss, and then within thirty days you

- Buy substantially identical stock or securities.
- Acquire substantially identical stock or securities in a fully taxable trade.
- Acquire a contract or option to buy substantially identical stock or securities.
- Acquire a substantially identical stock for your IRA or Roth IRA.

Of course, the functional phrase here is "substantially identical." In most cases, you can substitute the word "same" and get the same results, though the rule still applies in some cases where it isn't technically the same stock.

Here's an example: You buy one hundred shares of X stock for $1,000. They lose value, and you eventually sell them for $750. This is a capital loss of $250. If you were to buy one hundred shares of the same stock for $800 within the next thirty days, then you can't deduct that $250 loss from your other income. Additionally, you have to add your disallowed loss to the new stock to obtain your basis for tax purposes. In this case, it would be $1,050. That will also affect your capital gains computation at the end of the year.

Something similar happened to P. J.'s client Joseph Clark. In his personal, self-managed account, he purchased a position. Approximately one month later, he sold the position. This gave him a short-term capital loss of about $2,100. Then, Joseph repurchased the identical position within thirty days. This triggered a wash sale, which added $2,100 back to the new purchases, nullifying the STCL of $2,100. Ultimately, this meant that his taxable income was a couple of grand higher than he thought it would be because he wasn't aware of the rule.

So, if you're managing your own accounts, make sure you keep the wash sale rule in mind. Any account manager or advisor who handles your investments should be aware of the rule and avoid triggering it during their regular practice.

3. Municipal Bonds (Tax-Free Investment Options)

A final strategy to be aware of involves tax-free investment options. These investments are tax-free, as in the name, and so they're somewhat similar to tax-exempt retirement accounts like the Roth IRA.

Municipal bonds are an example of a tax-free investment option. Essentially, a municipal bond is a debt security used by cities, counties, or states to fund their expenditures. Because you're essentially lending money to the government, they come with a tax advantage. They aren't taxable at the federal level, and in most cases, they aren't taxable at the state level either.

So they help accredited investors and high-income earners earn tax-free income. These investors include Thomas Perez and Sarah White, clients who've worked with P. J.'s team. Thomas is fifty-four, and Sarah is fifty-five. They've used municipal bonds as a significant portion of their portfolio, and currently use them to generate tax-free income and growth.

In 2020, Thomas and Sarah's municipal bonds generated over $10,000 of tax-free income. P. J.'s team did the math on what that would look like if it were regular income according to their tax brackets and projected that going the route of municipal bonds saved them $3,700 in federal income tax.

Additionally, Thomas and Sarah worked with P. J.'s team to strategically harvest capital losses, much like Paul and Angela. In 2020, they managed to harvest $117,000 in capital losses, which of course offsets $117,000 in realized capital gains. According to the same projections, this saved them about $28,000 in federal income taxes.

If you're thinking about municipal bonds for your own portfolio, there are a couple that we recommend looking into. The first is the DFA Intermediate-Term National Municipal Bond Index Fund. These are short-term bonds owned in your portfolio, available nationwide. The second is the Vanguard Long-Term Tax-Exempt Fund. These are long-term bonds owned in your portfolio, available nationwide.

Investment Fees

We'll end with a note on investment fees. These are fees charged for contributing to certain funds at the point of transaction or distribution. In other words, you pay on the front end or the back end, depending on the fund. There are a few strategies for paying investment fees that can make a huge difference over years of investing.

If you have investment fees on your traditional IRA (or something where the distributions are taxable), pay any fees using the money from your distribution because it comes out taxable anyway. But if you have a back-end fee on your Roth IRA distributions, don't pay for them with your Roth IRA. This is because the Roth IRA income is nontaxable, so you want to hold onto it. Instead, pay the fees using your taxable income (and keep track of which is which).

 ## Chapter Summary

We've already discussed the importance of maxing out tax-advantaged retirement accounts. In this chapter, we took it a step further by encouraging you to gain an awareness of the tax rules for all of your investments. This way, you can actively manage taxes.

Your overall strategy could include working with a Dimensional Fund Advisor (DFA) managing a Separately Managed Account (SMA). This is a professional who actively manages your portfolio, strategically harvesting capital losses and building a custom portfolio that meets your needs.

We also talked about how wash sale rules are triggered, essentially when you buy a security after selling it for a capital loss. Plus, we suggested adding municipal bonds to your portfolio since the gains on them are tax-free.

Chapter Takeaways:

✓ If you have a high income or a high amount of front-end capital, consider working with a DFA to gain incremental growth and savings on taxes.

✓ Don't acquire a substantially identical security within thirty days of selling it for a loss, or it will count as a wash sale.

✓ Consider municipal bonds for your portfolio to generate tax-free income.

Strategy #4:

Make the Right IRA Contributions

We all have dreams when it comes to our finances and investments. This is one of the biggest reasons that people invest in the first place, for the hope that one day it will help some of their dreams come true. These could include things like traveling the world, opening a business during their golden years, or securing a legacy for their children and grandchildren.

One thing P. J.'s office does for clients is to take note of their dreams at the very beginning of the working relationship, and then help them get the financial means to make their dreams come true. It's always delightful to see someone's eyes light up when they get shown the math and realize that their dreams are possible.

That's also why P. J. and the team call IRAs the "dreams bucket." These include traditional IRAs and Roth IRAs.

Traditional IRA vs. Roth IRA

As we covered in Building Block #2, the difference between a traditional IRA and a Roth IRA is when you pay the taxes on them. With traditional IRAs, your contributions are deducted from your total taxable income on a yearly basis, saving you money here and now. For Roth IRAs, there is no tax benefit in the present, but your qualified distributions are tax-free.

In Strategy #2, we talked through whether one should prioritize tax-deferred or tax-exempt retirement accounts. Ideally, you will be maxing out some kind of tax-advantaged account on an annual basis, but whether it's an IRA or a Roth IRA depends on age, tax bracket, income sources, and preferences.

When P. J. works with a new client, his office often recommends that their adult children begin contributing the maximum to a Roth IRA as early as possible. Why? It's because they're younger, and they're usually in a lower tax bracket than their parents. Remember, if you're in a higher tax bracket, maxing out your 401(k) or traditional IRA could be a better move because it can push you into a lower tax bracket.

Because the money in a Roth IRA grows with compound interest, investing young starts the "Roth clock" early. The fund grows tax-free, and the qualified distributions are tax-free when the child eventually reaches retirement age. The younger the taxpayer begins, the more they'll feel the effects of compound interest. Ideally, they'll start as soon as they're eligible, maxing out their contributions the year they turn eighteen. This builds their dream bucket like none other. You can also begin a custodial Roth IRA for kids under eighteen; more on that in a moment.

However, not every eighteen-year-old has $6,000 in disposable income to max out their Roth IRA. This is where tax benefits for gifts come into play.

IRAs and Legacy Planning

Because of the benefits of the Roth clock, you should ensure your children begin healthy (if not maximum) Roth IRA contributions once they turn eighteen. Even if you're prioritizing a tax-deferred retirement plan yourself, you can still help them out with the gift exclusion.

This was something we also covered in Strategy #2, but we want to go into greater detail here and provide examples. What is the gift exclusion?

As of 2022, you can gift $16,000 as a single filer or married filing separately, or $32,000 for married filing jointly from your taxable estate. You can deduct this amount from your taxable income, and the recipient doesn't report it as income. Then, the recipient can use this gift to invest in a traditional IRA or Roth IRA, depending on their situation.

The following stories will help you make your own choices about gifts and IRA contributions:

Sarah Williams

Sarah Williams was in the 22 percent bracket in 2020 based on her income. When P. J.'s office began working with her parents, Martin and Christy, they asked about potential gifts. They determined that they could give an annual gift of $6,000 to Sarah for her to contribute to a retirement account. Remember, the limit (in 2020) for Michael to give would have been $15,000, and for Martin and Christy combined, it would have been $30,000.

Based on Sarah's tax bracket, P. J.'s team recommended contributing that $6,000 to a traditional IRA because it would lower her taxable income. This would reduce Sarah's projected taxes by $1,300, and of course, grow in the IRA over time.

Charles Martin

Charles and Karen Martin have two sons, Larry and Donald. When they began working with P. J.'s office, they determined that they could use the gift tax exclusion and give $6,000 to each son every year. Remember how the Roth IRA has a 2022 Adjusted Gross Income (AGI) limit of $129,000 per year for a single person? Both Larry and Donald were single and below that income threshold, so they could use that $6,000 to max out their Roth IRA each year.

This is similar to the story of John Sanders, the son of David and Lina. His parents gave him a gift of $30,000 each year, maxing out the joint gift exclusion. John used this to contribute to both a company-sponsored 401(k) and a Roth IRA. The former maximum contribution is $20,500, and the latter is $6,000, adding up to a $26,500 gift in 2022.

Andrew and Donna Martinez

The Martinezes have four children. In 2019, Parker was twenty-one, Barrett was twenty, Ivory was also twenty, and Jaden was seventeen. All of them had sporadic, part-time employment. Andrew and Donna decided to gift each child the *same amount* as their wages. This money went into a Roth IRA for the oldest three children and a custodial Roth IRA for their youngest, Jalen.

In 2019, each child managed to earn enough money for Andrew and Donna to gift them the maximum amount for their Roth IRAs, $6,000. If they continued to do so, then the Martinezes would keep on giving. This could be a fantastic way to teach your kids about retirement saving and incentivize them to start earning.

P. J. had talked about a similar plan with Franklin and Anika Reynolds in 2021. They have four children and four grandchildren. During initial planning, they suggested gifting up to the exclusion limit at that time of $30,000 ($15,000 from each parent, as of 2021) and dividing it among the children and grandchildren. They were thankful to have that information because they weren't aware of this potential strategy, which would allow them to gift up to $240,000 per year to their children and grandchildren without any tax consequences.

If you have children, consider employing one of the above strategies. If the child is young and/or in a lower tax bracket, your gift could go toward a Roth IRA. If they're in a higher bracket, then the gift could go into a 401(k) or traditional IRA. If you only have a few children or grandchildren and can max out your gift exclusion, then you could help your children and grandchildren max out both retirement accounts, as in the story of John.

Discretionary Income and IRAs

We'll end with the story of Joshua Davis. Some people work not because they have to, but because they want to. In other words, their income is entirely discretionary, not necessary, income. This often happens when someone is at retirement age or has a level of income or affluence from investments.

When P. J.'s team started working with Joshua, he was working part-time at the YMCA. He enjoyed the work and was making about $4,000 from that job annually. When P. J.'s team reviewed his finances, they discovered that he could contribute up to $7,000 per year of his wages into a Roth IRA because he is over 50 years old, to be withdrawn tax- and penalty-free whenever he needed it. Plus, even if Joshua started making a bit more, he could contribute more up to that $7,000 figure.

So, if you're in a situation where you have discretionary income, a similar contribution could be right for you. At the end of the day, we recommend maxing out a traditional IRA or Roth IRA, or getting as close as you can. If you're already doing that, consider getting a deduction by gifting money to go toward your children's and grandchildren's accounts.

With consistency, your dream bucket will continue to grow—until they all come true.

Chapter Summary

Everyone has dreams, and most of these dreams require money. Whether it's travel, a business idea, your legacy, or something else, contributing the maximum amount to an IRA could help you get there.

Whether you start contributing to a traditional IRA or a Roth IRA depends on your age, income sources, tax bracket, and personal preferences. Generally speaking, the younger you are and the less money you make, the more a Roth IRA will benefit you, and vice versa for the traditional IRA. Regardless, consider maxing one of those options out to support your dreams in retirement.

If you have enough disposable income, you could also consider gifting money to your children or grandchildren for their Roth or traditional IRAs. Most young people will benefit from starting their "Roth clock" early, but there are cases where a young person could benefit from contributing to a 401(k) instead.

Chapter Takeaways:

✓ Take the time to clarify your retirement dreams and what they might cost.

✓ If you can, contribute the maximum amount to a Roth or a traditional IRA annually. This becomes your "dream bucket."

✓ Some people have also cemented their legacy by gifting money for their descendants to invest into an IRA. This also confers a tax benefit to the donor.

Strategy #5:

Utilize All Available Retirement Plan Options

Kenneth and Carol Hall are a married couple in their late twenties. They have income from multiple sources, including W-2 employment. Kenneth also recently started a YouTube channel, and it took off. This caused him to start receiving large monthly cash flows from sponsors to his channel and income from YouTube directly. It also created a complex situation when it came to taxes and retirement planning.

Kenneth established a limited liability company (LLC) to mitigate his liability, but he didn't have a retirement plan yet. They weren't sure what the best options were because of the new cash flows on top of their existing W-2 income. What would the best retirement plan look like? Should they contribute to their workplace 401(k)s, set up Roth IRAs, or look for other options? Maybe they needed to try a combination of plans.

Similarly, you should review all the available options to see what's best for you. In this day and age, it's not uncommon to have multiple sources of income with tax structures, like with Kenneth and Carol. Plus, many of the people we've worked with are entrepreneurs by nature. This typically means multiple cash flows, some of which are irregular. If you're reading this book to gain the edge in your personal finances, chances are you have an entrepreneurial spirit too.

So how do you win at retirement planning with a complex income situation? Put differently, how do you maximize retirement contributions into various retirement plans in a way that decreases tax liability and grows exponentially?

This goes back to Strategy #2, maxing out tax-advantaged retirement accounts. Kenneth and Carol would probably favor the tax-deferred approach mentioned in that chapter. This is when people who land in a higher income tax bracket contribute as much as they can to tax-deferred retirement accounts. This way, they can push themselves into a lower tax bracket here and now and use the money they save however they like.

Some people take the money they save on taxes and put it toward tax-free retirement plans like Roth IRAs. It ultimately depends on the goals and dreams of the person or couple. Part of P. J.'s process is to discover the client's financial dreams and help them plan accordingly. In this way, the client reverse engineers their dreams and learns how much money to contribute to certain plans to get there.

This sometimes means taking an unconventional or combined approach. That's why we want to break down two less-traveled roads when it comes to retirement accounts: the Simplified Employee Pension (SEP) and the one-participant 401(k). Could one of these plans benefit Kenneth and Carol? Or you?

SEPs for Self-Employed People and Business Owners

A SEP is a Simplified Employee Pension. Employers can use it to pay into their employees' retirement. Some workplaces may offer it as a benefit: if you work here, we'll match your retirement contributions up to a certain amount or match part of your income.

Self-employed people can set up a SEP for themselves. In all cases, these contributions follow the same tax rules as a traditional IRA. Contributions are tax deductible now and taxed upon withdrawal. If you're the boss, you can set up a SEP at any time, possibly kicking in during your current tax year or the next one, depending on when you get your paperwork submitted and approved.

The SEP can be a fantastic option for those with multiple sources of income, or those who are self-employed and want to take a tax-deferred approach. They have higher contribution limits than 401(k)s and traditional IRAs. Remember, with a SEP, the business is the one contributing. The 2022 limit is either $61,000 or 25 percent of the net compensation of the employee, whichever is smaller. In 2021, the limit was $58,000.

Because these contributions are just like the contributions to an IRA for tax reasons, they count as a deduction from the business's total income at the end of the year. If you're self-employed, this could be extremely beneficial for your taxes each year.

Take the story of Amanda Walker. She's a real estate agent who works for herself. When Amanda began working with P. J.'s team, they had a meeting called the Tax Reduction Planning Meeting, or TRPM. During this time, P. J.'s team discovered that Amanda had a SEP, but she wasn't taking advantage of the tax benefits that would come from maximizing contributions.

So, P. J.'s team recommended that Amanda begin contributing the max to her SEP, which in 2020 was $57,000 or 25 percent of net income, whichever is less. Say that Amanda began investing the full $57,000 each year. With that plus all of her income, she'd write off that $57,000 and land in the 24 percent marginal tax bracket, instead of 32 percent. All said, it was a total projected savings of about $14,000 on her taxes. Plus, that $57,000 would begin compounding in her SEP. In 2022 and onward, Amanda can start investing $61,000 into her SEP.

One-Participant 401(k) Plans

Often called solo 401(k) plans, one-participant 401(k) plans are exactly what they sound like. They're a 401(k) plan for those who are self-employed or own a business without any employees. They have the same rules as a normal 401(k), except different rules when it comes to employer nonelective contributions.

In an employer nonelective contribution, the business can contribute up to 25 percent of the employee's total compensation in 2022. Total contributions from elective deferrals and employer nonelective contributions must not exceed $61,000, similar to SEPs above.

There's an additional beneficial wrinkle to the solo 401(k) that can help entrepreneurs greatly: self-employed individuals are both the employee and the one in control of the business, allowing them to contribute from their income and/or the business itself.

How Kenneth and Carol Benefited from a Solo 401(k)

P. J.'s office recommended that Kenneth establish a solo 401(k) and then maximize his employer contributions. This took $58,000 of his self-employed income from YouTube and sponsorships and contributed it. But wait, there's more: Remember how we said Kenneth and Carol each had W-2 income from other jobs? P. J.'s team also had them contribute the 2021 maximum to each of their workplace 401(k)s, $19,500 for each individual.

When all was said and done, their total retirement contribution was *$97,000 for the year.* In a 32 percent marginal tax bracket, they could save up to $31,000 in federal income taxes by deducting that $97,000. In addition to the team's recommendation for the money saved in Qualified Retirement Plans, P. J.'s team further recommended backdoor Roth IRA contributions for both Kenneth and Carol, with an additional combined $12,000 going into a tax-exempt account.

Why such an aggressive retirement plan? It comes down to two things: the client's dreams and the law of compounding returns.

For one, Kenneth and Carol began their relationship with P. J.'s team by dreaming about their Needs and Wants in the present and during retirement. This helped them determine how much money they would need at the outset of their retirement. Doing this allowed the team to determine how much would need to go into their retirement buckets, and when, to make that possible.

Time was also on their side. Because Kenneth and Carol are in their early twenties, their accounts will experience compounding interest. What does compounding interest mean? In this case, it means that the growth in their retirement accounts can immediately be reinvested and grow. This leads to exponential growth over a long enough period of time. So the $97,000 they invest in 2021 could be millions of dollars when they reach retirement age. Plus, when you add the $12,000 going into Roth IRAs (that comes out tax-free), the Halls will be able to make all their dreams come true during retirement.

You may want to begin your own SEP or solo 401(k). This is a fantastic option for self-employed individuals to make even greater contributions—and tax deductions—for their retirement.

 ## Chapter Summary

Besides the popular 401(k) and Roth IRA, there are other retirement plan options certain businesses are eligible for. These include the Simplified Employee Pension and solo 401(k).

P. J.'s team helped Amanda understand the benefits of maxing out her contribution to a SEP, which could help her save up to $14,000 in taxes each year while setting her up for retirement. The team also helped Kenneth and Carol Hall by recommending a solo 401(k) for Kenneth to invest his self-employed income. This enabled the couple to begin investing $97,000 into retirement in 2021, and more now that the limits have grown.

Chapter Takeaways:

✓ If you're an entrepreneur or self-employed, the SEP or one-participant 401(k) could help you contribute even more toward your retirement.

✓ These employer contributions are tax deductible, like contributions to any other tax-deferred retirement plan.

✓ The earlier you maximize your contributions, the better, due to the law of compounding returns.

Strategy #6:

Review Roth IRA Conversion Possibilities

Brian and Dorothy Harris are a married couple who want to minimize their tax liability in their retirement. They also want to avoid Required Minimum Distributions (RMDs) and the taxes that come with them. When they began working with P. J.'s office, the team discovered they already had significant savings in tax-deferred accounts. However, after crunching the numbers, P. J.'s team discovered a way to save them seven figures or more in lifetime taxes, through the power of a Roth IRA conversion.

This goes back to the premise of this entire book: Some people want to think about taxes as little as possible, and others simply try to get the biggest possible refund each year ... but these are the wrong goals. If someone wants to "win" at taxes, their goal should be to diligently strategize and find out how to lower their total lifetime tax obligations. The goal here isn't to get a bunch of money back from the IRS each year or outsource all the thinking to a tax preparer. The goal is to pay less in taxes throughout your life so that you keep most of your money. This enables you to have the retirement of your dreams and build your legacy.

For some people, the Roth IRA conversion is a perfect way to lower their lifetime tax obligations. However, it can cost them a bit on the front end.

What Are Roth IRA Conversions?

Roth IRA conversions are a planning strategy that allows repositioning assets from a traditional qualified retirement plan into a qualified Roth account. It requires the taxpayer to pay the taxes on the assets when they're withdrawn from the traditional plan.

If you get taxed when you withdraw your assets, why convert? It's because that's the last time you'll have to pay taxes on those assets. We covered the difference between tax-deferred and tax-exempt retirement plans in Building Block #2, but here's a quick refresher.

It comes down to when you pay the taxes on your contributions or distributions. In a tax-deferred plan, you don't pay taxes until you withdraw the money from your account. So the money you do contribute becomes a tax deduction, which lowers your taxable income and thus taxes.

When you do withdraw, your taxable income goes up because the distributions effectively count as income. If you have other income sources, or you've put away a significant amount, you could get pushed into a higher tax bracket by merit of retirement.

Tax-deferred plans also have the aforementioned RMDs, requiring you to distribute a portion of them every year after you turn seventy-two. We covered RMDs in more depth in Building Block #3. These essentially force you to withdraw your tax-deferred investments and pay taxes on them. This isn't the end of the world, but they should be a part of your overall plan for retirement.

In a tax-exempt plan like a Roth IRA, you don't get any benefits on the front end. If you make $60,000 and then put $6,000 into a Roth IRA, you can't write that contribution off. Your taxable income will remain $60,000. This is why some people in lower tax brackets prefer the Roth IRA. Not being able to deduct their contributions doesn't affect their effective tax rate as much as it would if they made more.

Plus, the qualified distributions of the Roth IRA are tax-free. You don't pay a dime on anything you withdraw once you hit retirement age (59½) and you've had the account for at least five years. There are also special provisions for withdrawing from the Roth IRA early, such as for a first-time home purchase or a medical emergency.

There's an additional advantage: Roth IRAs have no RMDs, meaning you can withdraw as much or as little as you like after retiring. The only time they become subject to RMDs is when they are inherited by someone who is not your spouse, when they are inherited by someone who is a nondesignated beneficiary, when your spouse is more than ten years younger than you, or if the account is still held by a 401(k).

Because of all this, some people perform a Roth IRA conversion to secure their legacy. The money in the Roth IRA can keep growing until the holder passes away, with no RMDs to shrink the investment. So the Roth IRA becomes an efficient way to transfer wealth to the next generation while eliminating the taxes.

When the designated beneficiary inherits the Roth IRA, they must withdraw all funds from the account within ten years of the decedent's death. In this way, you cannot treat Roth IRAs as a multigenerational trust. However, as long as the beneficiary has earned income to match a Roth IRA contribution, they could contribute to their own Roth IRA.

Note: As we covered in Building Block #4, each state has its own rules when it comes to taxes. It's no different for estate taxes. If you're thinking of using a Roth IRA to set up your legacy, you need to understand the rules for your state—and the states your children will live in.

Legacy planning isn't the only reason people convert, however. For many taxpayers, the lack of RMDs and the elimination of future tax liabilities are good enough reasons to switch. The lack of RMDs works well when you have other sources of income during your retirement too. This is because the Roth IRA will keep growing in the background. And even if you plan to give yourself regular qualified distributions when you retire, they are still tax-free and don't count toward your taxable income for tax brackets either.

A caveat: Converting to a Roth IRA can cause your taxable income to skyrocket the year you perform the conversion. That's something to be aware of and plan around. For instance, you don't have to perform the conversion all at once. In fact, P. J.'s office often advises clients to fill up their income bracket each year with Roth conversions, but not go over. This has a minimal impact on their effective tax rate and allows them to let a chunk of money begin growing tax-free each year.

Brian and Dorothy from the start of this chapter began this process with P. J.'s team in 2020. Brian converted $55,000 that year, for a projected future tax savings of $19,000. The next year, he converted $100,000 for a projected future savings of $39,000. Then, the team recommended that Dorothy begin converting on her own plan. Given their particular situation, if Dorothy converts $50,000 each year until it's all done in 2032, they'll save about $284,000 in taxes at the end of Dorothy's plan, at their current rate of conversion.

They could also decide to convert more aggressively. This means paying more in taxes on a year-to-year basis, but saving more when they retire. It all depends on the tax bracket they land in, or the one they want to fill up. Just a reminder: We covered tax brackets during Building Block #1. Your effective tax rate (the actual percentage of tax you pay) is most favorable when you fill up a bracket, but don't exceed it.

Remember, taxes can only do three things: Stay the same, go down, or go up. If you expect tax rates to increase over time, paying taxes now instead of later could help you tremendously. That's what Brian and Dorothy did. If they follow the plan P. J.'s team gave them, they're expected to save $1.4 million in taxes over their lifetime.

For those with multiple company-sponsored retirement plans, there's an even more effective option …

Check for Mega Backdoor Roth IRA Conversion Possibilities

Some company-sponsored retirement plans allow for mega backdoor Roth IRA contributions. This comes into play when the company offers both traditional and Roth 401(k)s. In this case, you can contribute a large amount to a traditional 401(k) and then transfer or convert it into the Roth 401(k).

Why do this? As we mentioned in Strategy #2, if your Modified Adjusted Gross Income (MAGI) in 2022 is over $144,000 for a single filer or married filing separately, or $214,000 jointly, you cannot contribute to a Roth IRA. There is also a way to simply pay more in taxes now, using a mega backdoor Roth contribution through your employer's qualified plan. The mega backdoor Roth allows you to save a maximum of $61,000 or $67,500 if you are age fifty or older in the qualified plan for tax year 2022.

In order to do a mega backdoor Roth IRA, your qualified company plan must offer both a qualified traditional option and a qualified Roth option, in addition to allowing the participants to make after-tax contributions.

First, make the maximum elective deferral into the company's qualified plan of $20,500 (per individual) and $27,000 if you are age fifty and older. You can then put an additional $40,500 of after-tax dollars into your qualified plan, assuming you don't get an employer match. However, if your company does offer a match to your contributions, you subtract that number from the $40,500 to arrive at your new total maximum contribution amount. All in all, the total limit for a mega backdoor Roth contribution is $61,000 or $67,500 if you are age fifty and older.

Remember, you have to pay taxes on whatever amount you convert from the traditional qualified plan to the qualified Roth plan. Plus, money you withdraw in less than five years will not be considered qualified distributions; they will be considered nonqualified distributions.

When done properly, it's a legal way to contribute well over the maximum amount you'd typically be able to contribute to a Roth IRA. It can even give people whose high income would normally prohibit them from contributing to a Roth the ability to do so.

P. J.'s team helped George Gonzalez with this in 2021. At the time, he was fifty-five. He was able to backdoor $38,500 in 2021 according to the 401(k) contribution limits of the time. Best of all, he only had to pay $26,000 into his 401(k) because of his employer's contributions. In 2022, he'll be able to backdoor up to $40,500.

We covered that this can be a good idea for those who don't need to use their retirement income during their retirement. George and his spouse are also contributing the maximum amount to pretax retirement accounts. Their backdoor Roth IRA fund can grow tax-free for their heirs, and they can use the RMDs from their tax-deferred account to live off. This smooths out their tax bracket now and will continue to do so during their retirement.

George and Brian will need to make sure all of these transactions meet proper bright-line IRS reporting requirements so they benefit from the tax-saving strategies outlined above.

Don't Forget About Form 8606

We touched on Form 8606 during Building Block #5, and here it merits further discussion. This is an annual form that is required to be completed to properly report any nondeductible IRA contributions.

If you don't file Form 8606, the IRS may assume those dollars converted from a traditional IRA to a Roth IRA were tax deductible. Therefore, by filing Form 8606, the IRS knows those contributions are nondeductible. You can then demonstrate to the IRS that a Roth conversion can be completed on a pro rata basis. So in future years, qualified distributions can be accurately accounted for as taxable or nontaxable income in the year of the distribution, thereby avoiding double taxation. For some of PJ's clients, this would be a seven-figure mistake.

So make sure you always properly report IRA cost basis to the IRS. If you're contributing to a Roth IRA, converting, or making backdoor contributions on a yearly basis, you should file an 8606 every year. This is on top of receiving Form 5498 from the account custodian, which goes for anyone contributing to an IRA, rolling accounts over, and making a Roth conversion. If you don't, you could get double taxed, which as we mentioned in Building Block #5, is the absolute worst way to tip the IRS.

Timothy and Deborah Lopez will have to do this for some of their distributions, unfortunately. When they began working with P. J.'s office, the team discovered they had neglected to file 8606 forms for after-tax contributions to each of their IRA accounts for the past seven years.

P. J.'s team filed Form 8606 to match their Form 5498s for each tax year, in addition to writing a letter to the IRS on behalf of the client with a detailed explanation of the prior year's 8606 that was not originally included in each tax year's return. This unreported nondeductible basis amounted to a total of $88,000 being resubmitted correctly. By accounting for the nondeductible IRA contributions made in prior years, Timothy and Deborah will not have to pay additional taxes on the future qualified distributions that include the $88,000.

If you stay on top of your annual tax reporting, your qualified distributions will be accurately taxed in the year of the distribution. Form 8606 completes this with the pro rata distribution method, whereas only the deductible portion of the distribution is taxed and the nondeductible portion is distributed tax-free. So upon qualified distributions, the IRS will know which dollars are taxable and which dollars are not taxable.

Ronald and Stephani Moore Benefited from Converting

The story of Ronald and Stephani Moore puts all these principles together. They're a married couple filing jointly who decided to work with P. J.'s team to maximize their retirement savings. When the pandemic hit, it created an economic trough. This was an opportune time to convert Stephani's IRA to a Roth IRA because it had lost about $14,000.

The basis in her IRA was $72,000, and the account value at the time of conversion was $58,000. So, when she converted, she didn't have to pay taxes on that conversion because she could write off the $14,000 in losses. They didn't stop there, however.

Ronald also converted $80,000 of his IRA into a Roth IRA, helping them fill up the 22 percent tax bracket and gain a projected future tax savings of $30,000. In 2021, they filled their bracket again by converting $100,000 for a future savings of $36,000. They plan to continue this strategy, or potentially convert at a more aggressive rate.

If they keep filling up the 22 percent bracket with their conversions, they'll end up converting about $684,000 over six years, for a potential tax savings of $236,000 after they retire. Because of tax-free growth and tax preferential treatment of their assets, their estate could be worth upward of $40 million.

Or they could choose to convert faster by filling up the 24 percent tax bracket. This would lead to more taxes here and now, but more tax savings at the end, due to more portfolio growth. P. J.'s team analyzes conversions and projections for clients every year, using the current tax code to mitigate future taxes and stretch assets further.

If you can convert to a Roth IRA, or even make backdoor contributions, then it could end up saving you hundreds of thousands in taxes after you retire. It requires paying taxes on the front end unless your IRA is below basis. However, all the money can be withdrawn whenever you like (or not at all) and grows tax-free. This is also a way to pass on your wealth to the next generation.

 ## Chapter Summary

A Roth IRA conversion can help you cement your financial legacy by reducing or eliminating taxes on money you pass to your heirs. It's ideal for this because it lacks Required Minimum Distributions and because qualified distributions are tax-free. Even if your legacy is taken care of by other means, the Roth IRA is preferable for some retirees because of its rules.

Converting to a Roth IRA requires paying taxes on whatever funds are converted from a traditional IRA in the tax year of conversion. To lessen the impact, some taxpayers convert enough to push them to the top of their tax bracket. Depending on their employer, they could also make backdoor Roth IRA contributions to exceed traditional contribution limits and to make higher income earners eligible for this tax-exempt retirement account.

Always make sure you clearly communicate all transactions to your tax preparer by providing all the proper forms. Form 8606 proves to the IRS that you already paid tax on your nondeductible contributions. Form 5498 will justify all of the contributions and activities that occurred in the specific tax year.

Chapter Takeaways:

✓ Consider converting to a Roth IRA, especially if you don't need its distributions during retirement and thus can use it for inheritance.

✓ If you work for an employer that offers both a traditional qualified plan and a Roth qualified plan, you may have the opportunity for nondeductible contributions and to make mega backdoor contributions over the usual limit.

✓ Make filing Form 8606 a requirement when making a nondeductible contribution and retain Form 5498 in your annual tax file. These can save you from double taxation and penalties.

Strategy #7:

Evaluate Low-Cost Variable Annuity Contributions

We mentioned the story of Thomas Perez and Sarah White back in Strategy #3, which was all about tax-aware investment. Their story also highlights another option for people wanting to put a significant amount away for retirement.

Thomas is fifty-four, and Sarah is fifty-five. When they began working with P. J.'s office, they had retirement at the top of their priority list. Their dream was to have enough cash flow during retirement to live the lifestyle they wanted.

To this end, they had both been maxing out contributions to their company-sponsored retirement plans for the past several years. These are like 401(k)s and 403(b)s, which we covered in Building Block #2 and Strategy #3. Remember, these retirement plans have Required Minimum Distributions (RMDs) that kick in after the taxpayer turns seventy-two.

So Thomas and Sarah want to have enough cash flow during retirement that their RMDs take care of their Needs and Wants, but to make this happen, they needed other cash flows as well. So P. J.'s team devised a plan to help them leave money in a nonqualified annuity.

Low-Cost Variable Annuity Contributions

Annuities are essentially savings vehicles that operate somewhat similarly to traditional IRAs. They're an opportunity for high-income earners who are maxing out traditional savings to save more and continue deferring taxes until retirement. These accounts come in two main forms: qualified and nonqualified. We'll explain the difference and demonstrate why Thomas and Sarah began contributing to a nonqualified plan.

First, the similarities. Both of these accounts are retirement plans, meaning you can't withdraw money from them until you are at least 59½ years old. If you do, you'll pay whatever taxes you owe and a 10 percent penalty on the distribution. For both plans, the earnings are taxed as ordinary income. The primary differentiator lies in the contributions, whether they are pretax or after-tax.

In a qualified annuity, contributions are pretax, meaning you can deduct contributions from your earnings that year and save on taxes. The investment still grows tax-free, but when you make qualified withdrawals in retirement, they're subject to income taxes. If that sounds familiar, it's because qualified annuities have similar tax treatments to Qualified Retirement Plans. These plans also have RMDs and contribution limits, like the ones Thomas and Sarah ran into.

For nonqualified annuities, the contributions are post-tax, meaning you can't deduct contributions from your earnings, but your principal investments are tax-free upon withdrawal. In this situation, you pay taxes on the gains. However, you don't have to make RMDs, and there is no contribution limit set by the IRS. So you can put in as much as you want and withdraw it tax-free at your own discretion during retirement.

So back to Thomas and Sarah's story. The nonqualified annuity was perfect for them because

- They were already maxing out their company-sponsored retirement plans. So they had the full tax benefit that comes from big contributions.
- They could live off their RMDs and other income sources after retirement, allowing the nonqualified plan to keep growing.
- Thomas and Sarah didn't qualify to put funds into a Roth IRA.
- They wanted an account that allowed them to make qualified withdrawals at their discretion after the age of 59½, or if dictated by the annuity contract.

If you have a similar situation, then you might consider a variable annuity yourself. In fact, Thomas and Sarah are far from alone:

The Thompsons' Story

We discussed Cody and Eleanor Thompson in Strategy #1 in relation to safe harbor rules. There are a few parallels between their situation and that of Thomas Perez and Sarah White.

For one, they're a similar age. Cody Thompson is fifty-one, and Eleanor is fifty-seven. They have similar retirement dreams to Perez and White, wanting to save more for retirement even after maxing out their traditional plans.

So when the Thompsons started working with P. J.'s office, the team recommended they begin contributing to a nonqualified annuity, just like Thomas and Sarah. As an example, if the Thompsons had nonqualified gains of $10,000 that year, it would save them up to $3,700 in federal taxes based on their marginal income tax bracket.

The tax-deferred status of the gains can also help the Thompsons out with state income taxes. As an example, when you rebalance your investments, the transactions will result in capital losses or capital gains. It is important to check the way your state taxes these kinds of gains so you can be prepared for any state taxes that might occur. Because the gains are tax-deferred in these annuities, asset allocation transactions do not create taxable gains at a federal or state level. So, if your state has additional taxes on capital gains, a variable annuity might be the move for you.

Chapter Summary

Variable annuities come in two primary forms: the qualified annuity and the nonqualified annuity. In the qualified annuity, contributions are pretax, grow tax-deferred, and are taxed as ordinary income when making qualified distributions. Qualified annuities are also subject to the IRS code for Required Minimum Distribution rules. In contrast, nonqualified annuity contributions are made with after-tax assets. There is no tax on the amount you pay into the annuity, but there is income tax on the growth when you take a qualified withdrawal. The IRS requires you to take the growth portion of the nonqualified annuity first.

Because of all these factors, a nonqualified annuity is a good opportunity for high-income earners to put away additional savings, especially if they're already maxing out traditional vehicles for retirement planning.

Chapter Takeaways:

✓ Consider a nonqualified annuity if you're maxing out all employer-sponsored contribution plans.

✓ Nonqualified annuities offer tax-deferred growth when the income is not needed, and you are in a high tax bracket.

✓ Nonqualified annuities tend to have more flexibility when it comes to qualified distributions and when marginal tax brackets may be reduced during retirement.

Strategy #8:

Consider Funding a Health Savings Account

We just talked about Cody and Eleanor Thompson in the last chapter. Their story also illustrates the benefits of a Health Savings Account (HSA), so it's worth recapping.

Cody (age fifty-one) and Eleanor (age fifty-seven) are targeting a retirement date of sixty-five years old. Because the Thompsons are high-income earners, they have been contributing the maximum amount to their respective employer-sponsored retirement plans, in addition to contributing to a nonqualified annuity. During a scheduled Tax Reduction Planning Meeting, it was discovered that Cody's current employer added an HSA option to Cody's list of benefits.

At this time, Cody's employer is making the maximum family contribution (2022 maximum of $7,300) on Cody's behalf. Because Eleanor is older than fifty-five, she has the option to contribute up to an extra $1,000. Eleanor's employer offers a High-Deductible Health Plan (HDHP) in which she can add her catch-up contribution of $1,000 to her separate HSA account.

Health Savings Accounts

So far, we've covered a number of retirement plan options. For an overview of your main options, refer to Building Block #2 and Strategy #3. However, we've only briefly touched on the HSA so far. It deserves an entire chapter because of the potential benefits.

HSAs are tax-advantaged and member-owned accounts that apply to those who have an HDHP, which can be an addition to those who are working and contributing to a tax-advantaged retirement account. If HSA funds are contributed through payroll, the funds are completely tax-free. The funds will then grow tax-free through interest and/or investments in the account and are tax-free upon the distribution of qualified medical expenses. Additionally, these assets never expire and can be used as a reimbursement for qualified medical expenses, even in prior years.

HSAs are a viable option for taxpayers to save extra money for healthcare needs when they retire. As you know, healthcare expenses tend to increase as we age, but not everyone plans properly for this. So the HSA helps people divert some of their pay into this crucial area. Plus, people can also make cash contributions to them for a slightly smaller tax advantage.

At the time of this writing, you can contribute up to $3,650 annually if you're single or married filing separately. If you're married filing jointly, you can contribute up to $7,300 in 2022. There's also a catch-up contribution rule, allowing you to put away an additional $1,000 after you turn fifty-five.

Many workplaces have an HSA plan that deducts the money for the HSA directly from payroll. In this instance, it's completely free of tax, including payroll tax. So contributing through payroll gets you the greatest tax-exempt benefit.

Within the HSA, the money can be managed and invested into funds of your choosing. When the assets are used for qualified medical expenses, they are distributed tax-free.

So it could potentially be the triple crown of tax-free savings vehicles:

- Your contributions are not subject to federal income tax. If they're deducted from your payroll, then they're free from payroll tax as well.
- The investments grow tax-free and benefit from compounding returns.
- When you use the distributions for qualified healthcare expenses, you don't have to pay taxes on them either.

Based on the tax savings, qualified dollars used on healthcare expenses from your HSA will go further than the assets being distributed from your IRA and will be taxed as ordinary income, making it a fantastic investment to add to your portfolio.

You can also contribute cash into an HSA, but you don't receive a deduction on payroll taxes in that instance. But you still don't have to pay federal and state taxes on them, almost as if they're contributions to a 401(k) or 403(b). That is, unless you live in California or New Jersey, which have special rules regarding your HSA contributions. (Please consult with your tax advisor and/or your state's Department of Revenue regarding HSA contributions.)

So once again, make sure you understand the tax situation of your state. We covered this back in Building Block #4, but it's worth reviewing. You need to know the tax rules of your state of residence and also be aware of the rules for any states you plan to move to when you retire.

How the Thompsons Benefited from HSA Contributions

Back to Cody and Eleanor Thompson. P. J.'s team saw that they only had one HSA, established through Cody's employer. This was good, but they weren't taking advantage of the maximum contributions and tax benefits.

P. J.'s team recommended that Eleanor should open an individual HSA account. Because she's over fifty-five, she qualifies for the catch-up contribution, adding $1,000 to her limit. Remember, the limit in 2021 was $7,200 for a family unless you could add the catch-up. So Eleanor started contributing an additional $1,000 into her own HSA account, adding to their total.

In this situation, Cody's workplace contributes $7,200 to his HSA as a benefit. However, if that wasn't the case, Cody could choose to have that money deducted from his payroll to be contributed tax-free. In that instance, since the HSA is potentially triple tax-free, their $8,200 contribution could save them up to $4,000 in current taxes.

Let's broaden the scope to Cody and Eleanor's lifetime situation: As of 2021, they have about $50,000 in Cody's HSA, and they have begun contributing $8,300 to max out their contributions in 2022 and onward. They're eligible to continue contributing to an HSA for more than a decade, until Cody turns sixty-five, or if they change from an HDHP.

After adding the family's maximum contribution and Eleanor's catch-up (until she turns sixty-five), they'll likely have more than $130,000 put away for healthcare expenses after retirement. This is before the investments grow whatsoever.

Once the Thompsons retire, they're projected to be in the 37 percent tax bracket based on their distributions and other sources of income, based on 2022's tax brackets. This is due to the large amount of money they've put away in traditional IRAs. Again, taxes could and likely will increase by the time they retire. At the least, the brackets could change.

So, when they withdraw money from their IRAs, the distribution is projected to reach up to the marginal tax bracket of 37 percent (2022 tax rates). But when they withdraw from the HSA toward qualified distributions, there will be zero (0 percent) tax to pay. This could save them upward of $61,000 in taxes depending on how much the accounts grow in the next few decades and what tax rates look like in 2037 and beyond.

If you begin this at a young enough age, you could have the entirety of your healthcare covered when you retire, and then some, as in the case of Dillon and Martha Mason's son, Kyle. P. J.'s team talked to Dillon Mason about the benefits of an HSA for him and his wife, Martha. They weren't eligible to fund HSA accounts, but they passed on the knowledge to Kyle.

He's twenty-two years old and unmarried. His mother advised him to begin the maximum payroll deduction to his HSA, which in his case is $3,650 in 2022. He won't reach age sixty-five for another forty-three years, so he can benefit greatly from the law of compounding returns. Even $3,650 invested now will be worth exponentially more in forty to sixty years. If Kyle keeps going with his payroll deduction, he could have multiple times what the Thompsons have when he retires.

A final note: An HSA shouldn't be your stand-alone plan. To get the full tax benefit, you need to use the money for healthcare, which is only one expense out of many after you retire. However, if you're eligible for an HSA, you should consider maxing it out. This money will compound and go further toward healthcare expenses than any other account can.

 ## Chapter Summary

A Health Savings Account (HSA) is a fantastic retirement investment to cover a much-needed expense for most retirees: Healthcare. Plus, it's one of the few accounts that can be contributed to and withdrawn from with absolutely no taxes.

To satisfy these requirements, the taxpayer needs to have a High-Deductible Health Plan (HDHP) established. If working, contributing through payroll deductions will maximize their tax savings (i.e., federal, payroll, state, local, where applicable). This will save them from paying income tax as well as payroll tax for the contributions.

Then, the assets will grow and compound tax-free in the HSA. If the assets are distributed to cover qualified healthcare expenses, then they are distributed tax-free. To sum up, this is an incredible way to cover healthcare expenditures without paying a dime in taxes.

Chapter Takeaways:

✓ Health Savings Accounts can be triple tax-free, saving you from payroll and income taxes, and they grow tax-free if you contribute and distribute correctly.

✓ Check whether your workplace offers an HSA and whether you can deduct some of your payroll into it.

✓ Even if you're not eligible, your children might be, and they can benefit more from the compounding growth.

Strategy #9:

Strategically Harvest Capital Gains

I n Building Block #2, we discussed tax brackets, namely the difference between income and capital gains tax brackets. Those rules are relevant here as well. Here's a brief summary:

The IRS uses a tax bracket for your income. It increases the marginal tax rate for your income at certain thresholds. It's a progressive system, meaning that you don't get taxed the same tax rate for all of your income, but only the income above each marginal tax bracket.

There's a different tax bracket for your capital gains, but it depends on your taxable income to work. It's also a progressive system, with the most notable bracket being 0 percent taxes for taxable income below $41,675 for unmarried individuals, $83,350 for married individuals filing joint returns, and $55,800 for heads of households in 2022.

However, don't be mistaken: The capital gains bracket is not independent of the income bracket. The 0 percent bracket only applies to your capital gains if your total taxable income is beneath that level.

For example, we shared the story of married individuals filing a joint return who earned less than that amount in a year, so they decided to harvest all their capital gains. They thought that since their income was less than $83,350, their harvests would be federally tax-free. But they ended up paying over $1,000 in taxes on what they harvested.

Other people think that all their capital gains beneath $83,350 will avoid federal taxes, which is also wrong. The money you take out as capital gains adds on to your income. This makes situations where harvesting only capital gains (and not also losses) is rarely advantageous for tax purposes.

However, there are situations where you can sell an appreciated asset without creating additional taxation. This mostly occurs in the instances where your total taxable income is beneath that $83,350 threshold. So your income and capital gains together don't exceed the 0 percent capital gains tax bracket.

This may happen if you are in a situation where your main income is withdrawals from a Roth account since they don't add toward your income. Or where you've made large tax-deductible contributions to a 401(k) or one of the plans we mentioned in Strategy #5—Simplified Employee Pensions and solo 401(k)s. In this case, your contributions can also lower your taxable income below the threshold. We'll cover the advantages of this and a couple of stories where it applied.

But first, take note: States have a variety of rules when it comes to taxing income and capital gains. Some states tax one and not the other, and some tax both. Most states recognize and tax capital gains at the state level, but there are several exceptions: Alaska, Florida, Nevada, New Hampshire, South Dakota, Tennessee, Texas, Washington, and Wyoming. Check your state rules before implementing this strategy.

If you do it correctly, it can help your tax situation in future years by resetting the cost basis of your investments.

Capital Gains and Cost Basis

Besides receiving money from your capital gains to either enjoy or reinvest, harvesting capital gains has another practical benefit for tax purposes: it resets the cost basis on your securities.

We talked about cost basis in Building Block #5. It is the total cost of a security, used for determining whether an investment appreciates or not. The cost basis is the price of the security plus whatever fees or surcharges get added, like investment fees.

The difference between the value of the security when you sell it and the basis becomes your gain (or loss). For tax purposes, losses can be extremely helpful. You can write them off to lower your taxable income, which we'll cover more in the next chapter.

If you have capital gains, it's because your investments have appreciated. So, if you sell them, you get an opportunity to buy them again at a higher cost basis. This would make it easier for you to harvest the losses later on. For tax purposes, a higher basis is generally more beneficial.

Two Stories of Strategic Gains Harvesting

Edward and Rebecca Anderson are a married couple who file jointly. They started working with P. J.'s office, and the team saw they had an opportunity to strategically harvest *long-term* capital gains.

What's the difference between long- and short-term capital gains or losses? It comes down to whether you've held the security for a year or longer. Short-term capital gains get taxed at the same rate as income, while long-term capital gains use the capital gains tax brackets. If you want a 0 percent tax rate on your capital gains, then you need to hold on to investments for a year or longer and reduce your taxable income to below $83,350.

For example, one year, Edward and Rebecca had a taxable income of about $40,000. So they could harvest up to another $43,350 in capital gains without creating capital gains tax. So the growth of these investments essentially came free of federal tax.

They did, however, realize a stealth tax on Social Security, which we'll cover in more depth in the next chapter. Still, they avoided federal income taxes on $43,350 of gains because they recognized they had the opportunity and took it. This is similar to an opportunity that P. J.'s team presented to Sharon Garcia.

Sharon began working with P. J.'s team and went through the standard Tax Reduction Planning Meeting (TRPM). There, the team discovered that if Sharon's income remained below $41,675 (the smallest capital gains bracket for an unmarried individual), then all qualified dividends and long-term capital gains would be taxed at 0 percent. Again, this is a good strategy for those whose Needs and Wants are covered by federally tax-free distributions, as in a Roth IRA. Or if they invested into a tax-deferred retirement plan and their Required Minimum Distributions haven't kicked in (or sit below that threshold).

Sharon's situation also brought up differences between states. P. J.'s team discovered that if Sharon's income remained below $50,000, then 65 percent of her Social Security income would not be taxable in her state of residence, West Virginia. Again, states have different rules when it comes to this. It goes to show the importance of working with a team dedicated to reducing your taxes, and the importance of understanding the tax situation of your state.

To sum up, harvesting capital gains under certain income thresholds will be exempt from federal capital gains tax. Some people reinvest this into the same securities to increase the cost basis, and others put it into a tax-exempt retirement plan like a Roth IRA. It depends on their overall retirement and tax strategy. This strategy can also be combined with strategic capital loss harvesting, which we'll cover in the next chapter.

Chapter Summary

Strategically harvesting capital gains can raise your income without raising your taxes. If you're married filing jointly, you typically need a total income (including the gains you just harvested) beneath $83,350. That's $41,675 for a single filer.

The assets you receive from realizing capital gains could be invested in the same securities at a higher cost basis. This could create an opportunity for capital gains tax loss harvesting if the investments depreciate in the future. If you have earned income to match potential contributions, you could also put it toward a tax-exempt retirement plan like a Roth IRA to generate more tax-free wealth later on.

Also, take the time to understand the income and capital gains tax brackets and how they interact. Some people have harvested significant amounts without realizing it would push them above the tax threshold. Lastly, your state may have additional taxes on capital gains for you to watch out for.

Chapter Takeaways:

✓ Make sure you understand the differences between the income tax and capital gains tax brackets and how they relate to one another.

✓ Each year, check whether you can harvest capital gains without increasing your federal income taxes. Pay attention to your state rules as well.

✓ These gains can be reinvested at a higher cost basis, making it easier for you to harvest losses later.

Strategy #10:

Strategically Harvest Tax Losses

Jeffrey and Alexa Lee are a married couple in their early 60s. Like many of the couples we've discussed so far, they wanted to set themselves up for retirement to cover all their Needs and Wants and also make their dreams come true.

When they began working with P. J., they seized the opportunity to sell some of their assets at a loss over the years and harvest the losses to offset future capital gains. Selling assets at a loss may seem counterintuitive from the outside looking in. After all, aren't you supposed to buy low and sell high?

If done correctly, harvesting losses can lead to a net gain financially due to the tax benefits that capital losses carry. This strategy can be implemented on its own or in tandem with the previous strategy, Strategically Harvest Capital Gains. The taxpayer can either use net losses for a tax deduction, and even carry losses forward into future years, or balance their losses and gains for a net-zero.

Background: IRS Revenue Ruling 74-175[5]

In 1972, a man who had a business sold off all his investments at a loss. This would typically count as a write-off for tax purposes, but the same year, he passed away. At that time, the tax rules stated that losses could be written off for the current tax year, but they didn't speak of what happened in the case of a death.

The IRS had to make a ruling about this regarding the estate. So Revenue Ruling 74-175 was born. It stated that the losses could only be used on the decedent's final tax return and could not be deductible by his or her estate or heirs. This expanded upon the IRS's ruling to allow tax loss carryovers on capital losses or net operating losses for business.

To sum up, you can carry your capital or operating losses forward into future years, but these losses stop being tax deductible the year you pass away. So taxpayers must make a plan to continually balance their gains and losses and/or exhaust their losses by the end of their lifetime.

Locking In Your Losses or Offsetting Gains

If you sell securities at a lower price than the cost basis you set when you bought them, it incurs a loss. You can sell the investments (at the reduced price), essentially locking in those losses. These losses can be used to offset gains in the same tax year. After the capital gains and capital losses have been netted out for the current year, the remainder of the capital loss can be carried forward to future years, offsetting capital gains. If there are no capital gains taken in a future year, the taxpayer can write off up to $3,000 worth of those harvested losses. This helps mitigate future taxes on capital gains that impact your income levels.

Or you can carefully balance your losses and gains to realize gains at no cost. It works like this: Capital losses offset capital gains, dollar for dollar. By selling just the right amount of losses and gains, you can balance them perfectly. In this case, your gains come to you without any

---

5   Bradford Tax Institute, "Rev. Rul. 74-175," Bradford Tax Institute, accessed July 14, 2022, https://www.bradfordtaxinstitute.com/Endnotes/Rev_Rul_74-175.pdf.

additional capital gains taxes because your net capital gains for the year are zero. Plus, if no gains are available in any given year, you can use up to $3,000 as a deduction on the current year's tax return. This lowers your taxable income, thus lowering your effective tax rate.

One strategy is to sell off one of your assets at a loss, and then replace it with a similar asset. This accomplishes two purposes:

1. You capture the loss. This locks it in for tax purposes. You can use the loss to offset other gains or to lower your total taxable income for the year. Then, you can also elect to carry losses forward into future years.

2. It also keeps your money invested in the market without creating a wash sale. We covered wash sale rules in Strategy #3, Tax-Aware Investment. Essentially, you can't buy back the same security or one substantially identical without triggering a wash sale, which resets the cost basis and disallows you from deducting the loss.

Special Rules and Considerations

There are a few special considerations that we've touched on so far and need to explain further.

Carryover

As mentioned previously, you can carry losses forward into future tax years. We discussed this in greater detail during Building Block #5. This requires meticulous reporting, but when done well, you can deduct losses each year until they are exhausted, reducing your taxable income significantly year over year.

Remember: Tax losses carried forward die with the taxpayer. You cannot harvest losses toward the end of your life and then pass them on to your heir for them to carry forward. So have a plan to exhaust them during your lifetime.

This benefited Jeffrey and Alexa Lee, whom we mentioned at the beginning of the chapter. As of 2021, they had over $295,000 in harvested losses to write off against future gains. By writing off the losses, they reset the cost basis of the investments and offset taxation from long-term capital gains. If done correctly, they could avoid taxation on over $950,000 in long-term capital gains over their lifetime.

They harvested these losses during the pandemic. This special circumstance gave many taxpayers the opportunity to rebalance their account without triggering additional taxation and allowed them to purchase assets in the "trough" of the market. So, as Jeffrey and Alexa sold off assets, they were able to harvest losses while reallocating assets to underappreciated assets in their portfolio while staying true to their predesigned asset allocation.

Social Security Stealth Tax and IRMAA

We touched on Social Security stealth tax in the last chapter, and here is the full discussion.

A stealth tax is a broad term used for taxes that the taxpayer isn't completely aware of. Or taxes that are not directly levied to the taxpayer even though they shoulder the cost. These are things like compliance and regulation for businesses, or sales tax. The business has to pay the tax, but they usually just raise their prices to make their customers pay for it.

Social Security has a stealth tax when your income lies over a certain threshold, though not everyone is even aware that they're paying it. This is because it isn't phrased as a tax per se because, as other sources of income flow to the tax return, it creates more taxable income on the Social Security benefit up to a maximum 85 percent threshold of the taxpayer's total Social Security benefit. Nevertheless, if your income is above a certain threshold, your Social Security benefits can be stealth taxed.

Single individuals with an income of $25,000 to $34,000 and married filing jointly with an income of $32,000 to $44,000 are taxed on up to 50 percent of their Social Security benefits. If your income exceeds those thresholds, you can get taxed on up to 85 percent of your Social Security benefits!

We mentioned the story of Dillon and Martha Mason's son during our discussion of Health Savings Accounts (HSAs) in Strategy #8. P. J.'s team recommended they use their harvested losses to counteract this stealth tax.

They recently retired, and they had an opportunity to sell assets at a loss, which generated about $113,000 in long-term capital losses. They plan to turn on Social Security when they reach age seventy and use their losses to reduce their taxable income during those years. This could also help them reduce taxes on future gains in their portfolio, of which they have $300,000 at the moment. This could also help them avoid or minimize Income-Related Monthly Adjustment Amounts (IRMAA) on Medicare.

Similar to Social Security, Medicare Part B enrollees have to adjust their monthly premiums when their income rises above a certain threshold. As of right now, married couples with a Modified Adjusted Gross Income (MAGI) of greater than $182,000 must pay an IRMAA in addition to their standard Medicare premium.

So Dillon and Martha could use their harvested losses to help keep their MAGI under the IRMAA threshold in retirement. Like the Lees, they also benefited from rebalancing their accounts during the pandemic, purchasing assets in the trough, locking in losses, and anticipating higher rates of return.

While downturns in the market can be emotionally stressful, confronting us with uncertainty, a downturn can potentially provide fantastic opportunities when rebalancing assets, adhering to the predetermined asset allocation. This strategy can in turn help potentially lower future tax obligations, even into and during retirement years.

Net Investment Income Tax

We'll cover Net Investment Income Tax (NIIT) in greater depth during Strategy #12, but here's a brief summary: NIIT is an additional tax of 3.8

percent for those with a MAGI above certain thresholds ($250,000 for married filing jointly) who also have investment income.

To avoid NIIT, you can reduce your MAGI or net investment income by harvesting losses. This presents another benefit to strategically harvesting capital losses. Saving 3.8 percent on your taxes can really help. Think of the case of Dillon and Martha with $300,000 worth of gains. A 3.8 percent tax would be $11,400. So check to see whether you might be liable for NIIT and consider reducing your MAGI under the threshold by deducting capital losses.

 ## Chapter Summary

Capital losses can be deducted from your income at the end of the year and carried forward into future years. This can be a way to reduce your tax obligations in a given year, or combined with capital gains, to offset the taxes you would need to pay on gains.

Some people strategically harvest their capital gains and losses to match them dollar for dollar. Others take a large loss and save it, to carry it forward into future years. This can help them avoid certain taxes in retirement, such as stealth tax on Social Security, Income-Related Monthly Adjustment Amounts (IRMAA) tax on Medicare Part B and Part D, and Net Investment Income Tax (NIIT).

Note: You can only use the losses incurred in your lifetime, so plan to exhaust them during your retirement at the latest. Also, although we didn't go into detail about this, because of a different rule, called the "wash sale rule," you should wait thirty-one days before repurchasing the same or an identical investment, or you will not be able to write off the loss, and the loss is added to the original cost basis of the investment.

Chapter Takeaways:

✓ Be aware of opportunities and consider balancing your capital gains and losses when applicable to your allocation and overall tax situation.

✓ You can also carry losses forward to help avoid certain taxes that come into play upon retirement, most notably Social Security for high earners.

✓ Make sure you have a plan to get the most out of all your losses during your lifetime because they cannot be used by your heir.

Strategy #11:

Review Income Shifting Strategies for Tax Bracket Smoothing/Leveraging and More

A ndrea Brown is a retiree receiving state pension, Social Security, and Required Minimum Distributions (RMDs) from a tax-deferred retirement plan. She started working with P. J.'s team to help manage her money and determine any ways by which she could reduce her taxes and make her retirement funds stretch further.

Andrea had a Tax Reduction Planning Meeting with P. J.'s office. In the meeting, they worked out a way to smooth her income tax bracket of 12 percent out through a Roth IRA conversion to help her money last longer and reduce her tax obligations when she finally withdrew it—or passed it onto her heirs.

The team recommended she begin shifting $10,000 of her traditional IRA income into a Roth IRA. This worked out because Andrea's other sources of income kept her marginally in the 12 percent tax bracket, even with the addition of the Roth IRA conversion. With Andrea's withholdings, she was able to shift the $10,000 into her Roth IRA and use those withholdings from her other income sources to offset any additional tax that would have been due with the $10,000 Roth conversion.

Multiple strategies we've covered so far have touched on the concept of tax bracket smoothing/leveraging. In Building Block #1, we covered the difference between marginal tax rate and effective tax rate. Marginal tax is how much tax you owe on the very next dollar you earn, based on your bracket. So, if your next dollar earned is in the 24 percent bracket, 24 cents of the dollar will go to Uncle Sam.

On the other hand, your effective tax rate is the average tax you pay on all your income. It's lower than your highest marginal tax rate. This is because the tax brackets work progressively. When you reach the 24 percent bracket, you don't pay 24 percent on all the previous money you've earned, just everything over that threshold.

So the effective tax rate looks like the average of all your income and capital gains brackets, after your deductions. Ideally, you should take steps to lower it as much as possible on a year-to-year basis or strategize ways to get the lowest effective tax rate over your lifetime, depending on your approach.

Mathematically, one of the best places to sit is at the tip-top of a tax bracket, but not over the line. If you graphed your effective tax rate, these points at the top of the brackets are points just before an upward curve. This is why we suggest filling up tax brackets and taking steps to ensure you can in future tax years as well. Plus, many of these strategies help you by utilizing tax-advantaged accounts.

There are multiple strategies to ensure you fill out your tax brackets and ensure your future tax brackets do the same.

Four Strategies for Tax Bracket Smoothing

Here are four strategies we recommend for tax bracket smoothing:

1. Roth IRA Conversions and Backdoor Roth Contributions

We talked about this in Strategy #6, with the story of Ronald and Stephani Moore. This is also what we recommended for Andrea Brown at the beginning of this chapter. Money from a traditional IRA can typically be converted to a Roth IRA and even exceed the normal Roth IRA contribution limit. The catch is, whatever assets you convert to a Roth IRA are taxed as income that year.

So some people can benefit from converting enough to fill out their current tax bracket. Then, the assets in the Roth IRA grow tax-free, and upon retirement they can be distributed tax- and penalty-free (with a qualifying distribution). Ronald and Stephani Moore started maximizing this strategy, converting $80,000–$100,000 each year into a Roth IRA and filling up their 22 percent tax bracket.

Additionally, if your workplace offers a traditional 401(k), Roth 401(k), and in-service nondeductible contributions, you can make a mega backdoor Roth contribution, as mentioned in Strategy #6. This involves contributing assets from your Roth 401(k) at a higher contribution limit than the normal Roth IRA. Plus, you can still do this even if your Modified Adjusted Gross Income (MAGI) is too high to make regular Roth contributions.

This strategy creates tax-deferred growth during your high-income-earning years, no RMDs, and tax-free legacy planning. If it's a possibility for you, look into it! You could make backdoor Roth contributions to smooth out your tax bracket, just like a normal Roth conversion.

2. Capital Gain and Loss Harvesting

We covered these in Strategy #10. You can harvest your capital losses to offset potential future realized gains. Or, as in Strategy #9, you can harvest capital gains when you know you'll remain in a low marginal tax bracket, thus paying 0 percent in federal taxes on them.

You can also strategically harvest losses and gains to smooth out (or drop down) your tax bracket. For example, a married filing jointly couple could harvest enough capital gains to take them to $83,350 in taxable income each year, and not over. Or a couple who slightly exceed a tax bracket threshold could use their losses to reduce their taxable income and bump themselves down.

3. Nonqualified Annuities

Nonqualified annuities were the subject of Strategy #7. These are non-qualified retirement accounts that have special rules. They are often used by those who max out traditional retirement accounts.

In a nonqualified annuity, you don't receive a tax deduction for the assets you contribute. The investments grow tax-deferred, and when it's time to retire, the money you originally invested isn't taxed. Only the growth is taxed. Plus, nonqualified annuities don't have RMDs.

These annuities can't necessarily help you during your working years with tax bracket smoothing. However, they do defer growth and allow you to save a significant amount during your working years.

The tax bracket benefits come after retirement age. Because there is no RMD, you can strategically distribute from your nonqualified annuity each year any money you need for your Needs and Wants, without paying taxes on it.

Note: You will pay taxes on the gains of a nonqualified annuity, which are taken into account first when you withdraw them. It's a last-in-first-out system for distributions, and the principle is tax-free.

4. Charitable Remainder Trusts

We'll cover these in greater detail in Strategy #17, but here's a brief overview:

If you have significantly long-term appreciated assets, you can contribute these assets to a Charitable Remainder Trust (CRT). When the trust sells them, they are exempt from taxes. It shifts the capital gains tax of the highly appreciated asset to the CRT, avoiding significant taxation.

Committing assets to the trust counts as a charitable contribution, enabling you to lower your taxable income and perhaps slide down to the top of a bracket. This is a good strategy for those who have held onto their assets for a very long time.

Quarterly Estimated Payments

Lastly, we talked about quarterly estimated payments in Strategy #1 during our discussion of safe harbor rules. It's worth rehashing them here, to ensure you don't get hit with any additional penalties.

During the tax year, income can be recognized in specific quarters to avoid penalties. The most common instance where this is necessary comes from business income. Many people investing through a business need to pay special attention to this.

If you try any of these strategies for tax bracket smoothing, pay attention to how it will affect your quarterly income and adjust accordingly. It could be worth working with a tax expert on a quarterly basis for this, to make sure you don't run into penalties that offset whatever tax savings you were getting.

 ## Chapter Summary

Smoothing out your tax bracket can help you get the lowest possible effective tax rate on your income. To make this happen, many people find ways to adjust their taxable income to fill up their current tax bracket or shift down to the top of the previous bracket.

Strategies for this include Roth IRA conversion (including possible backdoor Roth contributions), capital gain and loss harvesting, contributions to nonqualified annuities, and Charitable Remainder Trusts.

Additionally, having income from so many sources often requires you to report your income throughout the year in quarters, instead of all at once at the end of the year. Make sure you don't get hit with surprise penalties because the IRS expects you to declare income on a quarterly basis and apportion the income tax accordingly with estimated quarterly payments.

Chapter Takeaways:

✓ Check whether you could benefit from any of the four strategies listed above.

✓ Performing just one strategy, or combining them, could help you achieve a lower effective tax rate in addition to saving for your retirement.

✓ Also check whether you need to make quarterly estimated tax payments. This is often the case when you have business income, a structured entity for investments, or you have unexpected extra income (i.e., a Roth conversion).

Strategy #12:

Minimize Net Investment Income Tax Obligations

D r. Jacob and Kathleen Robertson are forty-three and forty-two respectively. They're high-income earners, looking for ways to put away money for the retirement of their dreams. Their marginal tax bracket is on the high end at 37 percent, so they want ways to invest without running up a large tax bill either at the time of contribution or distribution.

To get to the retirement of their dreams, the Robertsons have a significant obstacle to overcome: Net Investment Income Tax (NIIT). We touched on NIIT during our discussion of tax loss harvesting, and it deserves a section of its own.

NIIT is an extra tax on individuals who have both Modified Adjusted Gross Income (MAGI) over a certain threshold and investment income from certain sources. NIIT doesn't just apply to individuals but also to estates and trusts.

You're potentially liable for NIIT with a MAGI over the following threshold amounts in 2022:

- Married filing jointly or qualifying widow(er): $250,000

- Married filing separately: $125,000
- All other cases: $200,000

This tax applies to income from certain investments, including

- Interest
- Dividends
- Certain annuities
- Royalties
- Rents or other sources of passive income
- Stock options
- Capital gains

So, if you fulfill both of the above conditions (MAGI and investment income), you'll owe NIIT. How much will it set you back?

NIIT is a 3.8 percent tax on the lesser of

1. Your net investment income
2. The excess of MAGI over your threshold

So, if you make $20,000 above the threshold for your category, but your net investment income is $10,000, you'll owe $380 in NIIT. Remember, this is in addition to income tax and capital gains tax, so it can add up quite quickly … especially for those with a significantly high income, high investment income, or both.

Note: NIIT also applies to income derived in a trade or business wherein you have a passive role, or a business that trades in financial instruments or commodities, or one that has net gains from the disposition of property. To sum up, there are few investments immune to NIIT once your MAGI goes over the threshold.

So what did P. J.'s team recommend for the Robertsons? They needed something with tax-deferred growth so that the gains wouldn't be subject to taxes until they retire and sit in a lower income bracket. Preferably, they needed something that allowed them to invest as much as they needed.

If you've been following along at home, you may have guessed "nonqualified annuity," and you're correct. P. J.'s team recommended that Jacob and Kathleen immediately begin investing in a nonqualified annuity to shelter the capital gains and dividends. If they kept investing in taxable accounts, then all the gains and dividends would be subject to the extra 3.8 percent—or worse, their income would get taxed directly.

If your income is over the threshold, consider investing in a nonqualified annuity yourself. You can also prove that your business income isn't coming passively but actively through material participation, but that's trickier. Here's how:

Material Participation

If you qualify as a material participant in a business, then the income from that business isn't classified as investment income, but as income. You must meet certain criteria to prove that the income isn't passive, but nonpassive (or active). This could help you avoid NIIT by recategorizing your income, but it only works in certain cases.

> Here are the criteria for proving material participation in a business, taken directly from IRS Publication 925:[6]
>
> 1. You participated in the activity for more than 500 hours.

---

6   U.S. Department of the Treasury, Internal Revenue Service, *Publication 925 (2019), Passive Activity and At-Risk Rules*, IRS, accessed July 14, 2022, https://www.irs.gov/publications/p925.

2. Your participation was substantially all the participation in the activity of all individuals for the tax year, including the participation of individuals who didn't own any interest in the activity.

3. You participated in the activity for more than 100 hours during the tax year, and you participated at least as much as any other individual (including individuals who didn't own any interest in the activity) for the year.

4. The activity is a significant participation activity, and you participated in all significant participation activities for more than 500 hours. A significant participation activity is any trade or business activity in which you participated for more than 100 hours during the year and in which you didn't materially participate under any of the material participation tests, other than this test....

5. You materially participated in the activity (other than by meeting this fifth test) for any 5 (whether or not consecutive) of the 10 immediately preceding tax years.

6. The activity is a personal service activity in which you materially participated for any 3 (whether or not consecutive) preceding tax years. An activity is a personal service activity if it involves the performance of personal services in the fields of health (including veterinary services), law, engineering, architecture, accounting, actuarial science, performing arts, consulting, or any other trade or business in which capital isn't a material income-producing factor.

7. Based on all the facts and circumstances, you participated in the activity on a regular, continuous, and substantial basis during the year.

There are multiple paths to getting to material participation, but as you can see, they require forethought, strategy, and documentation. Some investors have found success by grouping together their business activities, thus consolidating their efforts into one business and making material participation easier.

If you want more help with material participation, we strongly recommend working with an expert to ensure proper strategy and documentation.

How the Lewises Avoided NIIT during Their Work Years

Let's end with another example of avoiding NIIT. There are two main strategies to getting past NIIT that depend on your income situation and retirement savings approach. The first is to simply lower your MAGI to beneath the threshold. This can be done by maxing out your tax-deferred retirement accounts, like we mentioned in Strategy #2. You could also lower your MAGI through charitable contributions, deductions, and benefits.

However, some people still have too much income to fall beneath the threshold, even when they max out tax-deferred contributions (or elect for a different investment approach). Jonathan and Anna Lewis fall into this category. They were extremely high-income earners while Jonathan was working, pushing them over the $250,000 threshold. Still, they wanted to avoid NIIT so they could make the most out of their investments.

P. J.'s team recommended that, like the Robertsons, they invest money into a nonqualified annuity (to read more about these accounts, check out Strategy #7). As mentioned previously, investments in a nonqualified annuity defer the taxes on all growth until retirement. This means that the investment income cannot be taxed until withdrawal. Plus, the original contributions can't be taxed at all since they get taxed along with your income each year.

Now, Jonathan and Anna are retired. They're in a lower tax bracket, beneath the minimum threshold for NIIT. They've begun to draw income from the nonqualified annuity. These accounts have no Required Minimum Distributions, so the Lewises can use as much or little of it as they need.

The growth from their nonqualified annuity gets taxed each year because it counts toward their taxable income. However, the original contributions don't get taxed at all. Plus, because their MAGI now falls below the NIIT threshold, they don't have to worry about that extra 3.8 percent tax.

Chapter Summary

Net Investment Income Tax (NIIT) is an additional tax for taxpayers who have their net investment income above certain thresholds. You're subject to NIIT if you have net investment income and your Modified Adjusted Gross Income (MAGI) is above $250,000 for married filing jointly or $125,000 for married filing separately.

There are two main ways we recommend avoiding paying NIIT. The first is to prove material participation in a business generating income subject to investment tax. NIIT applies to passive income, so proving material participation makes the income nonpassive.

The second way is to invest in a nonqualified annuity. In these plans, all the growth is tax-deferred, lowering your taxable income and avoiding tax until after you distribute the income in retirement.

Chapter Takeaways:

✓ Determine whether you might be subject to NIIT by looking at your MAGI and comparing it to the thresholds.

✓ See if you can prove that you are a material participant in a business generating investment income to avoid or minimize NIIT.

✓ A nonqualified annuity could help by deferring taxes on your investment growth until after you retire.

Strategy #13:

Consider Bunching Strategies for Itemized Deductions

So far, we've covered strategies for saving income and shifting it to avoid or minimize tax obligations. However, there's another side to not getting killed on taxes, which involves maximizing benefits and deductions. This lowers tax obligations on a year-by-year basis.

We laid the groundwork for this during Building Block #5, which was all about capturing every benefit you're entitled to. The main point from this building block? Document everything!

Make sure you have a system in place to capture every benefit you're entitled to. Keep a tax spreadsheet that you can add to each year and save the receipts to confirm evidence of anything that could count as a deduction. You're entitled to the tax benefits that come from your itemized deductions. They belong to you. However, the IRS won't beat down your door to remind you about them.

Standard and Itemized Deductions: The Story of Dan and Rosette

Going into greater depth, there are two options ahead of each taxpayer (or married couple filing jointly) each year. They can either take the standard deduction or report itemized deductions.

The standard deduction is used when the itemized deductions do not exceed the standard deduction. Most people take this when they can't make enough itemized deductions or don't want to make the effort to report all their itemized deductions. However, with the right strategy, you can alternate which deduction to take to minimize your tax obligations.

For 2022, the standard deduction is $12,950 for a single filer or $25,900 for married filing jointly. For our purposes, let's create a hypothetical married couple, Dan and Rosette. They're a young married couple, enjoying matrimonial bliss and preparing to win at taxes over their lifetime. Smart move.

Let's say they claim the maximum annual real estate and state income tax deduction of $10,000, and they have $6,000 in mortgage interest that they can deduct. You see, Dan and Rosette just bought a house together. This adds up to $16,000 in deductions, which is still well below the standard threshold of $25,900 … $9,900 below to be exact. To get up to the standard deduction, they're in need of $9,900 in charitable contributions that year, or more if they want to benefit from itemizing.

Let's say this couple makes about $4,000 in charitable contributions each year. That won't get them to the standard deduction. Here, they have two options. One, they could take the standard deduction each year and enjoy the $5,900 reduction in their taxable income. However, this isn't a long-term strategy that takes multiple years into account. They could instead bunch their charitable contributions for several years into one year, and then itemize. If they did four years of charitable contributions at once, that would be $16,000, enabling them to itemize for a deduction of $32,000 instead of the standard $25,900. For the next three years, they could take the standard deduction, rinse and repeat. They could also alternate every other year between itemized and standard deductions, depending on their preferences and long-term strategy.

Deduction bunching is a good way to lower tax liability in a given year. If your income is significantly different from one year to the next, then you should bunch and itemize during the years your income is larger.

Note: Cash gifts are limited to 60 percent of your Adjusted Gross Income (AGI) for deductions, according to the current tax law. So this couple probably wouldn't be able to bunch and itemize ten years' worth of charitable contributions without reaching the limit. That's why it's best to alternate in shorter intervals.

Going Further: Donor-Advised Fund Investments

You can take this strategy a step further with Donor-Advised Funds (DAFs), which carry additional benefits besides helping you exceed the standard deduction in certain years. DAFs are a form of tax-preferenced investment account, specifically earmarked for charitable giving. Contributions are treated like a gift to a 501(c)(3).

There are several advantages to opening a DAF:

- You receive tax deductions to your contributions during the year you contribute. This presents the same flexibility as the strategy above.

- This, in turn, helps even out spikes in income, enabling you to exceed the standard deduction in the year of your choosing and lower your taxable income.

- Because the money is managed in a central fund, you can donate less in years with tighter income, and it won't necessarily hurt the charity.

- You can give anonymously or create an "In Memoriam" fund.

- Having such a fund could help you teach charity to your children, and even create a family legacy of giving through your fund.

- Because the fund is donor-advised, you can evaluate the charity's fiscal responsibility over time, with enhanced visibility. This could help you make decisions about future donations, or help you decide whether you want to shift to a different charity.

We've talked about Paul and Angela Corbin a couple of times throughout this book. They're the high-income earners who wanted to make sure their investments were socially responsible. They also have a complex income landscape, with W-2 income and passive income that can fluctuate greatly on an annual basis.

Paul and Angela want to invest and donate responsibly and pass on a charitable legacy to their children. In addition to setting up a socially responsible investment portfolio, P. J.'s team also recommended a DAF. This will accomplish their dream of leaving a charitable foundation for their children while smoothing out spikes in income.

For instance, during a year when Paul's passive income is higher, they often land in the 37 percent marginal tax bracket. During these years, Paul and Angela can bunch their donations to reduce their tax exposure. This assists the charities of their choice while diminishing their tax liability.

For example, if they land just above the 37 percent marginal tax rate threshold, they could decide to make a $50,000 donation to their DAF. This will reduce their marginal tax rate from 37 percent to 35 percent and reduce their overall tax liability by $18,500 for the year.

If you think you will consistently bunch your itemized deductions on an irregular basis like Paul and Angela (or Dan and Rosette), consider starting a DAF. This will help you lower your tax liability, but also leave a positive legacy and an example to future generations.

 ## Chapter Summary

Itemized deductions are a way to reduce your taxable income, thus lowering your tax liability. However, some people simply try to deduct the maximum amount they can each year without a long-term plan in mind.

For those with income that fluctuates significantly year to year, they should consider bunching their itemized deductions in the years with higher income, to reduce their marginal tax rate. This can be done by making several years' worth of donations in one year, if one is charitably inclined. These methods can also be employed to reach the standard deduction threshold in a given year.

A related method involves setting up a Donor-Advised Fund (DAF) for charitable giving. Then, one can donate more or less in a given year to the fund to even out spikes in income. This is also a way to give while gaining visibility into the charity's fiscal responsibility, to set up a legacy of giving, and to teach one's children about generosity.

Chapter Takeaways:

✓ If you have an income that spikes from year to year, consider bunching your charitable contributions or other itemized deductions in the same year your income spikes.

✓ This could reduce your marginal tax rate and could help you reach the standard deduction threshold in a given year.

✓ To enhance this, consider contributing to a DAF as a vehicle for contributions.

Strategy #14:

Manage Medicare (IRMAA) Brackets

Like many of P. J.'s clients, Mark and Pamela Chang are a married couple who want to make the most out of their retirement. Mark retired in 2021, but while he was employed, the Changs mostly fell in the 24 percent marginal tax bracket.

Once Mark retired, their taxable income decreased. This put them in a lower tax bracket, but since his income was higher just before he retired, he was liable for a substantially high Medicare premium. This happened even though his income is lower now. They began working with P. J.'s team to determine a way to manage their income-related adjustments. Thankfully, there are a variety of strategies one might employ before and after retirement to help.

We've discussed how having a high income during retirement could cause a couple of stealth taxes to hit you, namely an extremely high tax on Social Security distributions and higher Medicare premiums through Income-Related Monthly Adjustment Amounts (IRMAA). However, your income just before retiring factors in as well.

The Medicare premiums are based on rules about IRMAA and are based on your income from the past *two years* and operate on a sliding scale. When your Modified Adjusted Gross Income (MAGI) is higher, it makes the premiums higher for Medicare Part B (Medical Insurance) and Part D (Prescription Drug Coverage).

Since Medicare operates on a two-year look back in regard to your Medicare premiums, your MAGI in the year you retire is not the only part of the equation. For high-income earners who retire and experience a significant drop in income, like Dr. Chang, this can be a substantial unnecessary cost. There are a couple of ways to lower IRMAA premium costs for retirees, one of which helped the Changs significantly.

SSA-44

Due to Medicare's look back of two years in regard to Medicare premiums, Mark and Pamela Chang used an SSA-44 form. If you want the full name (and it's a mouthful), this form is known as the "Medicare Income-Related Monthly Adjustment Amount - Life-Changing Event" form.

It's used to request a reduction in your IRMAA adjustment on the basis of a major life change. It can be used in incidents where one of your major sources of income suddenly vanishes or gets reduced significantly. Some categories of life-changing events include (but are not limited to) divorce or annulment, loss of income-producing property, or work stoppage.

When Dr. Chang's income levels decreased, P. J.'s office recommended they complete an SSA-44 form to report it. Their premiums beforehand were $297 for Part B and $31.80 for Part D. After filling out the form, their premiums dropped to $207.9 and $12.30 respectively.

If they hadn't filled out the form, they would have continued paying inflated premiums in 2021 and 2022 before the look back could recognize Mark's lower income levels. If you have a similar situation (or a different life-changing event), then look into the SSA-44.

QCDs

Qualified Charitable Distributions (QCDs) are a tool we touched on during Building Block #3. We'll cover QCDs in depth in the next chapter, but for now, know that they're a strategy that could lower your MAGI and thus reduce or eliminate IRMAA.

A QCD is a donation straight from your tax-deferred retirement account (i.e., an IRA) into the charity of your choice. Since you don't report the QCD distribution as income, it can't raise your taxable income for the year. This method works best when you have income from other sources. Still, because it can lower your taxable income, it's something to look into if you want to minimize IRMAA.

Capital Loss Harvesting

We covered capital loss harvesting in Strategy #10. It's a means by which you can lower your taxable income, by strategically deciding when to deduct your capital losses. It requires some planning and documentation on the front end.

To reduce your IRMAA, utilizing capital loss harvesting that carries forward to future tax years can offset future capital gains, thus keeping a reduced IRMAA premium during harvesting years. Carrying forward net capital losses through harvesting is just another strategy to make the most of during Medicare years.

So, if you know you'll be facing a Medicare IRMAA increase after you retire, consider harvesting capital losses now and saving them. This could potentially eliminate Medicare adjustments entirely or reduce your IRMAA from year to year if your losses are great enough or your taxable income during retirement is low enough.

Roth Conversion

Lastly, we covered Roth conversions in greater detail during Strategy #6, and they're a brilliant front-end strategy for avoiding additional taxes during retirement.

You can convert traditional IRAs to Roth IRAs at any time during your career. This causes you to effectively distribute the IRA, pay taxes on it, and then put it into a Roth IRA. This is also a workaround for the Roth IRA contribution limit. If you're an exceptionally high earner, and your workplace has the right plans, you can also make backdoor Roth contributions from your employer-sponsored 401(k) to an employer-sponsored Roth 401(k).

Many people combine this strategy with tax bracket smoothing, which we covered in Strategy #11. Jonathan and Anna Lewis benefited from this. During a tax planning meeting, P. J.'s team analyzed the Lewises' investments and cash flows to help them plan for retirement.

The team then recommended a $70,000 Roth conversion to fill up the Lewises' current income bracket of 22 percent, without crossing the Medicare bracket floor level. Jonathan will apply for Medicare in 2022 and Anna will apply in 2024. Because they have started putting away these funds into a tax-exempt retirement plan, it won't count toward their taxable income during retirement.

This is projected to save the Lewises up to $900.65 in IRMAA adjustments for Jonathan's Medicare Part B and D. When Anna applies, it could save them even more. The Lewises simply had to pay taxes on the front end when they made the conversion to save on them drastically during retirement.

To sum up: If you haven't retired yet, consider the Roth IRA conversion or a year when you can harvest significant capital losses to carry over. If you're retiring soon, think about using Form SSA-44 to report a significant decrease in income due to work stoppage. If your Needs and Wants are covered outside your traditional IRA, consider turning your distributions into QCDs to lower your MAGI, minimize or avoid IRMAA, and provide a distribution to a valued charity.

Chapter Summary

Income-Related Monthly Adjustment Amounts (IRMAA) brackets, which are based on the two-year look back, can cause substantially higher and unnecessary increases in Medicare Parts B and D premiums. Due diligence and careful analysis of income should be forward-looking and reviewed on an annual basis leading up to the Medicare years.

To mitigate or avoid these adjustments, the taxpayer can lower their taxable income through Qualified Charitable Distributions, capital loss harvesting, and the reduction of Required Minimum Distributions through Roth conversions in prior years. They can also fill out Form SSA-44 for a chance at reducing their premiums.

Chapter Takeaways:

✓ Determine now whether you might have to make higher Medicare payments upon retirement.

✓ If so, consider harvesting capital losses or converting some of your retirement funds to a Roth IRA to counteract this.

✓ If you're already retired, filling out Form SSA-44 and/or making Qualified Charitable Distributions can provide a reduction in your annual Modified Adjusted Gross Income.

Strategy #15:

Evaluate Possible Qualified Charitable Distributions (QCDs)

Jackson and Emma Hill are a retired couple who made significant capital gains in 2020. This was projected to increase their Required Minimum Distributions (RMDs) and push them into higher Medicare premium brackets. Not good.

They began working with P. J.'s team to find ways to reduce their tax obligations and continue the retirement of their dreams. This led to a Tax Reduction Planning Meeting, wherein P. J.'s team recommended QCDs, or Qualified Charitable Distributions. Because the Hills are charitably inclined, this became a fantastic method to fund their chosen social causes, save money in federal taxes, and reduce their Medicare Parts B and D premium costs.

Jackson and Emma ended up donating about $7,000 from their tax-deferred retirement account, allowing them to save $1,500 in federal taxes based on their bracket. Likewise, while you have an opportunity to financially and emotionally benefit from QCDs, the charity of your choice monetarily benefits from your generosity.

A QCD is a nontaxable distribution to an organization eligible to receive tax-deductible contributions. These distributions effectively become donations, sent from your retirement account to the charitable organization. If you are charitably inclined, you can use QCDs as a tax mitigation strategy to lower your taxable ordinary income below certain tax thresholds. All in all, it's a helpful strategy for those who are not able to itemize tax deductions and have significant assets in tax-deferred accounts.

Benefits and Guidelines for QCDs

Besides possibly saving on federal taxes, Social Security stealth tax, and healthcare premium costs during retirement, you can also use QCDs to satisfy RMDs. We talked in depth about RMDs during Building Block #3. They are a means by which the IRS ensures you pay taxes on your tax-deferred retirement savings, requiring you to distribute a portion of your funds each year after you turn seventy-two. Because RMDs are distributions from a tax-deferred retirement account, they increase your taxable income for that year. By utilizing the QCD strategy, assets are distributed from the tax-deferred accounts directly to the charity of choice, thus avoiding a taxable event for the taxpayer.

Thankfully, you can turn your RMDs into QCDs. You can donate up to $100,000 per taxpayer as a Qualified Charitable Contribution and exclude it from your taxes. You can also donate more, but you will have to report it and pay taxes on it, so it's best to avoid that unless your RMDs are well over that mark.

Again, for those unable to itemize deductions, donors receive an immediate tax deduction with a QCD, thus further lowering your taxable income. If you'd like a refresher, we discussed itemized vs. standard deductions in Strategy #13.

In addition to the maximum annual exclusion of $100,000, you have to be at least 70½ to make a QCD. This dovetails nicely with the age at which RMDs kick in, which is the year after the taxpayer turns seventy-two.

In addition to the Hills, Scott and Nicole Green also benefited from QCDs. They had a Tax Reduction Planning Meeting with P. J.'s office, in which the team discovered that they were taking their RMDs as a lump sum. They were considering QCDs in addition to this. The team showed the Greens that to reduce taxable income, the QCD should come directly from their RMD income.

The net effect of this is a reduction of taxes through a contribution to a qualified charity from the taxpayer's RMD. So the Greens began planning to use their QCD strategy in conjunction with RMDs in future years, which reduced their federal tax liability, minimized Social Security stealth taxes, and reduced their Income-Related Monthly Adjustment Amounts (IRMAA) premium to the base bracket. This worked because their Needs and Wants were already covered outside their RMDs, and they had a desire to give money to charities close to their hearts. If you have a similar situation to the Hills and Greens, then regular QCDs could be the right move for you.

 ## Chapter Summary

Qualified Charitable Distributions (QCDs) are tax-exempt donations to charitable organizations made directly from your tax-deferred retirement account. They are a strategy used to possibly lower your tax obligations and can be extremely effective during Required Minimum Distribution (RMD) years, while contributing to an important charity the taxpayer cares for.

Utilizing a QCD strategy, starting at the age of 70½, can help possibly lower your taxable liability and extend your generosity by helping a charity of your choice. The maximum amount you can exclude from your income is currently $100,000 per year. This strategy is deployable when your needs bucket has been satisfied by other forms of income.

Chapter Takeaways:

✓ If you are investing heavily into a tax-deferred retirement plan, consider making QCDs a part of your overall retirement strategy.

✓ QCDs benefit the charity of your choice and possibly lower your taxable income, helping you potentially lower Social Security stealth tax and Medicare IRMAA premiums.

✓ When deploying QCDs from within your RMDs, your tax mitigation strategy will be most effective.

Strategy #16:

Gifting Strategies to Reduce Overall Tax Obligations

Remember Thomas Perez and Sarah White? We've discussed their story off and on throughout the book, but here's a quick recap. Thomas is fifty-four, and Sarah is fifty-five. They wanted to take advantage of tax-advantaged investing opportunities to maximize their dreams going into retirement. Ideally, they wanted to do this while lowering their tax obligations, so that they could make sure their dreams and wishes were funded.

Besides their traditional investments, they invested into a municipal bond to generate tax-free income. They also used a nonqualified annuity to increase their retirement savings above the limit outlined by a traditional 401(k). Because of the high level of investment into an IRA and a nonqualified annuity, they have over $800,000 of long-term capital gains in their joint account.

Thomas and Sarah are in the 37 percent marginal tax bracket. Since distributions from a nonqualified annuity count as ordinary income, and they already sit in a high long-term capital gains bracket, they are looking at a huge tax on any of their distributions.

To help offset the capital gains in their taxable joint account, P. J.'s team evaluated gifting strategies with them, which developed into a strategy to gift money to their three children every year. This would accomplish two of their biggest goals: to lower their tax obligations during retirement and set their children up for success.

In 2021, P. J.'s team recommended they begin gifting highly appreciated low-cost-basis assets from their joint account to each of their children up to $30,000 for a total asset gift of $90,000.

As we covered way back in Strategy #2, the annual gifting exclusion in 2021 was $15,000 for a single individual, or $30,000 for a married couple filing jointly. That's why Thomas and Sarah can gift up to $90,000 in assets each year to their three children ($30,000 to each child), while still remaining below the annual gift tax exclusion. This strategy allows the taxpayers to shift long-term capital gains from their high tax bracket to their children's low tax bracket in conjunction with fulfilling their gifting strategy.

Once the child receives the gift, they can then sell the appreciated asset realizing capital gains in the lower tax bracket, and in turn, fully fund a company-sponsored retirement savings plan through their wage earnings and/or fund an Individual Retirement Account (traditional or Roth IRA) up to $6,000 or the maximum their wage income can support.

Is Gifting Gains Right for You?

This strategy worked well for Thomas and Sarah because they had purchased equities at a low cost and held their position over time, leading to huge capital gains. This could mean high taxes if they wanted to harvest those gains. Because so many people harvest their long-term capital gains during retirement, they experience a large increase in Adjusted Gross Income, leading to a stealth tax on Social Security and increased Income-Related Monthly Adjustment Amounts (IRMAA) premiums, which we covered during Strategy #10.

However, this couple didn't need to rely solely on their capital gains for income during retirement. They could donate the securities to their children and fulfill their Needs and Wants through other means.

In this instance, the donee receives the security at the donor's cost basis, and the donor loses control of the asset once gifted. If the position is sold, then the donee is liable for the capital gains tax liability to possibly include what other taxable income they may have, including state taxes. Gifting highly appreciated positions will also reduce the value of the donor's estate for tax purposes. However, to reduce the estate, this has to be done three years before the donor's death. If the gifting occurs within three years of the donor's death, it will be considered a "deathbed gift" and count as part of the estate.

To sum all that up, gifting gains might be right for you if

1. You have gifting intentions.
2. You don't depend on the long-term capital gains for your retirement income.
3. You want a way to reduce your tax obligations.
4. The recipient of the gift will have taxable income of under $83,350 (2022 rates).
5. You are likely to live longer than three years.

Noncash Charitable Contributions

Besides gifting appreciated securities, you can also gift noncash assets to reduce your tax obligations. This will allow you to increase your itemized deductions each year, in turn reducing your tax obligations proportionally based on your marginal tax bracket.

For example, Cody and Eleanor Thompson donated a vehicle worth $2,400 (Fair Market Value) that was subsequently sold. This gave them a charitable deduction on the cost of the vehicle, ultimately reducing their taxes by about $900 for that year.

Here's an additional story: Amy King donated clothes, furniture, and household items with a Fair Market Value of about $7,200. Since Amy is in the 35 percent marginal tax bracket, this saved her $2,500 in federal taxes and about $750 in NY state and city taxes.

Individuals, partnerships, and corporations need to file Form 8283 to report information about noncash charitable contributions if the amount of their total noncash gift deduction is over $500. Plus, for their yearly filing, the taxpayer needs to file a Schedule A with their return.

If you have a vehicle, furniture, or expensive clothes and jewelry, consider turning it into a noncash charitable distribution for a tax deduction. This asset could go to a beneficiary like a child or a charitable organization and subsequently be sold to raise money for their cause.

Donating Appreciated Stocks to Charity

Lastly, you can also donate appreciated stocks to charitable organizations, rather than donating the assets to your children. If you're in a similar situation to Thomas and Sarah and have long-held equities that've appreciated dramatically over the years, this could be the right move for you.

When you donate appreciated stocks to charity, the charity inherits your cost basis on the security. So the Fair Market Value of the security on the date of donation is the donated value for you, the donor.

Eric Youngkin benefited from this. Eric is currently in the 24 percent marginal tax bracket and has appreciated stocks that he doesn't need for his retirement income. So P. J.'s team advised him to combine the donation of $30,000 in appreciated stocks to a charity and use the itemized deduction. As a refresher, we covered itemized versus standard deductions in Strategy #13. This strategy helped Eric get a projected tax deduction of about $7,200 on his annual filing.

Remember to itemize your deductions on Schedule A to claim the tax deduction benefit. Donate stocks that have appreciated, so you can avoid capital gains tax, but don't donate stocks that have depreciated. You can harvest those losses for a similar deduction, like we discussed in Strategy #10. If you still want to donate a stock that has lost value, consider the following strategy:

1. Sell the asset at a loss and claim capital losses.
2. Use that loss as a deduction or to offset gains made elsewhere.
3. Donate the cash from the sale to help the charity and give yourself a charitable contribution deduction.

Chapter Summary

During retirement age, using the aforementioned strategy can help reduce marginal tax dollars to the taxpayer's desired level. There are multiple gifting strategies to employ for those who have a high level of taxable investments and assets.

Taxpayers can use their unrealized capital gains by gifting them to the donee of their choice or to charity. This will make the recipient inherit the cost basis and gain control of the security. An heir could reinvest this money while realizing capital gains at a lower or tax-free rate. Donating stocks to charity will allow the donor to deduct the gains from their taxes while benefiting their chosen charity.

One can also make noncash charitable contributions. This allows the taxpayer to deduct the Fair Market Value (FMV) of the asset for tax savings.

Chapter Takeaways:

✓ If you have appreciated investments and assets, consider gifting strategies to reduce your taxable income. This can be especially helpful if you're retired and want to leave a legacy.

✓ Gifting strategies can provide other avenues for donees to increase their retirement assets (i.e., 401(k), traditional IRA, and Roth IRA contributions).

✓ Another way to lower your taxable obligations is through gifting noncash assets for a deduction at the FMV of the asset.

Strategy #17:

Using Charitable Remainder Trusts to Reduce Tax Obligations

Charitable Remainder Trusts (CRTs) are somewhat similar to other gifting strategies, but they come with special rules. We touched on them during Strategy #11 about shifting income to smooth out tax brackets. To understand their specific use, let's share a story.

There's another couple working with P. J.'s office. Let's call them John and Mary Smith. John and Mary have been investing in the stock market throughout their working years. Their stocks were purchased for $50,000 total, but now they've appreciated to a value of $400,000. Those long-term capital gains come with a significant amount of taxes if they wish to sell those stocks for retirement income.

In the Smith's current bracket, they would pay a 15 percent tax on capital gains. Since $400,000 (the value) minus $50,000 (the investment) is $350,000, that number represents their capital gains. If they sold everything today, they'd need to pay 15 percent on the gains, for a whopping bill of $52,500. This means the $400,000 they have is really worth about $347,500 for their retirement.

Plus, the Smiths still own the assets. This means they have no protection from creditors, and no deduction for charitable contributions using the money. They could donate the appreciated stocks to charity, like we discussed in the last chapter, and realize a tax deduction from the appreciated, unrealized gain by the charity.

Instead of harvesting the gains and paying capital gains taxes, they have another option: transferring the stocks to a CRT.

Charitable Remainder Trusts

What are CRTs? These are accounts that one party transfers (or trusts) to another to hold. The recipient must use the money for the direct benefit of others, hence the "charitable" part of the name. These trusts help taxpayers lower their taxable income and estate taxes and leave a positive, charitable legacy.

CRTs are designed to help estate tax liability and support charities. They also could help with tax bracket smoothing, as mentioned previously. Unlike simply donating the stocks directly to a charitable organization, they come with financial benefits for the donee, beyond just receiving a donation, such as being able to avoid federal income taxes if they realize the gain of the stock within the zero percent capital gains income tax threshold.

The best type of assets to transfer to a CRT are highly appreciated, low-income assets like real estate and stocks, especially stocks of closely held corporations. The property in the CRT can't be encumbered debt. Once the assets are transferred, the trustee diverts income back to the trustor (or grantor) on a regular basis.

A CRT will generally benefit the trustor for up to twenty years or until they pass away, by giving them designated income from the trust. This income can also be diverted to another beneficiary if the trustor so chooses. After the dispensing period is over, the remainder of the trust goes to the charity/charities of the trustor's choice. There are multiple rules regarding contributions and distributions depending on the type of CRT. Here are the three basic types:

1. A Charitable Remainder Annuity Trust (CRAT)

The CRAT pays a fixed stream of income to a designated beneficiary, like John and Mary. Once the beneficiary passes away, the remainder of the CRAT passes to a charity designated by the grantor. CRATs can only be contributed by the grantor once, and assets cannot be added after that initial contribution. However, the income from the trust will not change regardless of the trust's performance on the market.

If you want to create a CRAT, it's best to use cash or readily marketable assets to fund it. Since it's a onetime contribution, it's advisable to make it as large as possible.

2. Charitable Remainder Unitrust (CRUT)

In a CRUT, the donor receives a fixed percentage of the trust's assets annually, instead of a fixed income amount. Because of this, the annual income will fluctuate. In this type of CRT, the assets will grow tax-free. Instead of making a onetime contribution, the donor can continue to make multiple gifts over time.

3. Net Income with Makeup Charitable Remainder Unitrust (NIMCRUT)

Try saying that name three times fast! In a NIMCRUT, the donor doesn't receive any income for a set period of time (e.g., fifteen years) until they take constructive receipt of the income. This income will go into a holding/IOU account for bookkeeping purposes. When the donor decides to begin receiving the income, they receive a percentage of income from the trust, like in the CRUT. This trust is helpful for tax purposes on the front end, but it's a gamble. If the beneficiary passes away before accessing their holding/IOU account, then all the assets go to the designated charity as usual.

When to Create a CRT

With the story of the Smiths and the types of CRT in mind, we can determine a set of criteria for this decision. Create a CRT if you

1. Have highly appreciated assets and wish to avoid capital gains tax
2. Are charitably inclined
3. Want to generate retirement income
4. Wish to lower taxes on your estate

All of these reasons fit John and Mary's story. As mentioned before, they have $350,000 of gains liable for taxes. If they transfer their stock to a CRT instead, they can take an immediate charitable contribution tax deduction, based on IRS Schedule A, Itemized Deductions. Then, the trust will control the stock, but because the trust is exempt from capital gains tax, the full $400,000 is available to reinvest.

John and Mary are charitably inclined. One of their retirement dreams is to use some of their money to fund causes close to their heart, thus leaving a legacy of generosity. They also wanted to generate retirement income for themselves with their appreciated assets, and so they didn't want to donate everything right away.

Lastly, because the assets are now in an irrevocable trust, they are protected from creditors. The asset is no longer a part of the Smith estate, and therefore not subject to estate tax. If you have a similar situation or story, then creating a CRT might be the right move for you.

Remember Ronald and Stephani Moore? We discussed their situation during our section on Roth IRA conversions in Strategy #6. They have approximately five thousand six hundred shares of Apple stock, which have appreciated over time.

During a strategy meeting with P. J.'s team, one of our Financial Wellness LifeCoaches recommended they transfer the stock into a CRT, similar to the recommendation for the Smiths. This would give them an immediate charitable income tax deduction on top of allowing them to benefit from the asset without tax liability. The trustee could then sell the shares in Apple and reallocate them to potentially reduce market risk.

If the Moores opted into a CRAT, they would then receive a fixed income each year until they pass away. When that day comes, the rest of the money will pass to a designated charity.

As you can see, the CRT forms a hybrid between donating to charity and selling. It sets up an irrevocable trust that will benefit the charity of your choice after you pass away. At the start, it gives you a charitable contribution deduction, or an annual deduction if you choose the CRUT. Then, it grows tax-free and grants you regular retirement income.

Chapter Summary

A Charitable Remainder Trust (CRT) generates retirement income for the trustor(s) while giving them a tax deduction. It additionally reduces the estate tax of the trustor(s) since the assets go to designated charities after the dispensing period. Typically, retirees open CRTs toward the beginning of their retirement with highly appreciated assets like real estate and stocks.

The benefits of CRTs include lowering taxable income, granting a charitable contribution deduction, avoiding capital gains taxes, and leaving a charitable legacy. Depending on your retirement strategy, they can be a fantastic way to supplement your retirement income.

Chapter Takeaways:

✓ Consider a CRT if you are charitably inclined and have highly appreciated, long-held assets.

✓ A CRT will lower your tax liability estate taxes after you pass on.

✓ There are three main types of CRT, so make sure you choose the one best for your situation and preferences by consulting with a qualified estate attorney who is knowledgeable about this estate planning tool.

Strategically Using 529 Plans to Save for Education While Minimizing Taxes

G regory and Christine Turner are a married couple who want to reduce their tax obligations and manage their money well. They began working with P. J.'s office toward the end of 2020. Like many of the couples we've covered so far, they want to live comfortably in retirement with the means to cover their Needs, Wants, and Dreams. They also want to leave a legacy for the next generation.

As mentioned before, one of the crucial components at the beginning of working with DiNuzzo Wealth Management is a Tax Reduction Planning Meeting, or TRPM for short. The individual or couple meets with tax planners who obsess over the details, finding ways to save them money on taxes. From there, they develop a strategy that helps the client meet their financial and retirement dreams while taking advantage of as many tax-reducing strategies as possible.

During the TRPM with Gregory and Christine, P. J.'s team discovered that they weren't taking advantage of a relatively obscure tax deduction because they weren't aware of their state's rules. The Turners had invested $10,000 into what is known as a 529 plan the prior year … but they hadn't claimed the benefits for it. Thankfully, addressing this benefit is part of the TRPM checklist.

In the Turner's state of Pennsylvania, there's a state income tax deduction for qualified contributions to these plans. Gregory and Christine weren't aware of this benefit. So, after P. J.'s team discovered it, they amended their 2020 tax return to get the PA tax deduction of $307. Going forward, they know they can claim that tax deduction every year they contribute to these specific plans.

What Are 529 Plans?

A 529 plan is a tax-advantaged savings plan designed to encourage savings for future education costs. It is also known as a "Qualified Tuition Plan." Distributions from these plans can be used to cover educational expenses such as tuition, board, and textbooks. Many of them are sponsored by states, state agencies, and educational institutions. Because of the specific usage of the distributions, they often carry tax benefits. This isn't dissimilar to Health Savings Accounts earmarked for medical expenses, like we covered in Strategy #8.

Of course, when we think of education expenses, many people think of postsecondary education like colleges and universities. However, qualified distributions also include K–12 expenses. This means tuition for private schools and the supplies that parents need to buy each year. Depending on your tax strategy, 529 plans could be contributed to and distributed from in the short term, for short-term tax benefits … or they could be allowed to appreciate over time, to cover more educational expenses for a child's university education.

There's a special rule for contributions to these plans: They're dictated at the state level instead of the federal level. Every state has its rules regarding eligibility and aggregate limits. For example, in P. J.'s state of Pennsylvania, contributions are allowed up to $511,758 per beneficiary.

If the account (or multiple accounts) accrues to $511,758, then contributions are no longer available to be made.

Several states offer tax deductions on qualified contributions. Because these deductions are offered at the state level, they are deducted from state income tax. So you can't use a 529 plan deduction on your federal income tax return.

Additionally, if your state doesn't have income tax, then you may not benefit as much from contributing. Still, contributions are considered gifts since they go toward someone else's education. Therefore, you can use them toward maxing out your annual gifting exclusion for federal tax deductions.

Some states offer parity as an added incentive for you to contribute. These include Arizona, Arkansas, Kansas, Minnesota, Missouri, Montana, and Pennsylvania. If you reside in one of those states, like Gregory and Christine, you have an additional incentive to contribute.

An additional strength of these plans is the variety of qualified distributions. A 529 plan allows up to $10,000 to repay qualified student loans (lifetime limit). Plus, Registered Apprenticeship Programs now count as qualified distributions, meaning your child doesn't need to go to a four-year school after their secondary education to benefit.

Lastly, most 529 plans can be transferred to a sibling or certain other beneficiaries. This could happen if the child no longer needs the distributions for any reason, as in the case of getting a full-ride scholarship to their university.

When to Invest in a 529 Plan

With all those factors in mind, whether the 529 plan makes for a good strategy depends on a few factors. Contribute to a 529 plan if you

1. Have children whose educational expenses are not covered by grants and scholarships

2. Desire to fund a portion or all of your child's or other beneficiaries' higher education needs through a tax-advantaged investment strategy

3. Reside in a state that offers in-state 529 plan tax benefits, and your beneficiary will use the distributions in that state

4. Reside in a state that offers parity for 529 plan contributions regardless of the beneficiary's state

5. Need additional ways to max out your annual gifting exclusion

Here's another example, from the story of Ronald and Stephani Moore. We discussed in the last chapter how they could create a Charitable Remainder Trust to generate retirement income and avoid capital gains taxes.

They also expressed a desire to help fund their daughter's master's degree. While they live in Pennsylvania, their daughter is going to school in Massachusetts. Her master's degree will cost approximately $20,000 after grants and scholarships. Because the Moores live in Pennsylvania, P. J.'s team recommended they open a 529 plan and receive a Pennsylvania tax deduction. After all is said and done, they would receive a deduction of $614 from their state income taxes.

Remember, your tax rules will vary from state to state. This was the subject of Building Block #4, and it has come up in every strategy that includes state tax rules. Ronald and Stephani live in one of the seven states that offer the option to give this benefit regardless of where their beneficiary goes to school. Check on your own state's rules about income tax and 529 plan benefits to be safe before investing.

Additionally, look at the lifetime contribution limits for your state plan because they vary. Some states also have a per-beneficiary limit instead of per-contributor. For example, in Pennsylvania the lifetime limit per beneficiary is $511,758.

We mentioned Andrew and Donna Martinez back in Strategy #4 about IRA contributions. They decided to match the contributions of their four children into Roth IRAs to increase their gift exclusion while setting up their legacy. On top of this, they decided to take full advantage of the benefits of the 529 plan offered in Pennsylvania.

In 2021, Andrew and Donna contributed $150,000 for each of their children ($75,000 per spouse), up to Pennsylvania's total contribution limit for a single year. This "super funding" gave them a Pennsylvania tax deduction of $3,684, since they maxed out their gift exclusion of $30,000 per child.

Plus, the gift could be spread out over five years for federal income tax purposes by filing Form 709 per donor (United States Gift Tax Return), allowing them to claim the maximum gift exclusion each year just for their 529 contributions in 2021.

Andrew and Donna's story is a case study into how state and federal tax rules interact. Generally speaking, the taxpayer will get the best benefits if they reside in one of the seven states that offer 529 tax deductions, regardless of the beneficiary's state. Their story and the others in this chapter, also demonstrate that there is almost always a tax benefit to be found when you give your money toward your child's education and/or retirement.

 ## Chapter Summary

A 529 plan is a savings account specifically designed to help pay for education costs. Many people invest in a 529 plan to fund postsecondary education for their children, as it can be used for tuition, board, and books. However, it can also be used for K–12 education expenses, as well as apprenticeship programs.

States have varying rules and regulations regarding 529 plans. Some offer parity, and some offer tax deductions on state income tax for contributions. They also have a range of aggregate contribution limits. Therefore, this strategy's utility can vary depending on one's state of residence.

Chapter Takeaways:

✓ Determine the rules regarding 529 plans for your state to see if it's right for you.

✓ If so, this can be a fantastic way to fund the education of your children or beneficiaries while getting a tax benefit.

✓ You could also use it for K–12 education and apprenticeship programs.

✓ You are able to use up to $10,000 to repay qualified student loans.

✓ A 529 plan offers another avenue for gifting strategies for loved ones.

Strategy #19:

Using the S Election to Save Employment Taxes

While most of the previous strategies have included stories from P. J. and his wealth management office, the last two are special strategies courtesy of Steven. They offer a window into special rules taxpayers can take advantage of to save.

The first in the lineup is S election, a strategy that helps business owners save on employment taxes. To understand this strategy better, we need to back up and discuss payroll taxes at large.

If you weren't aware, payroll taxes are withholdings of pay that go to the IRS. They come in addition to normal federal and state income tax. Payroll taxes are used to fund special programs that we've already talked about, like Social Security and Medicare.

There's a common misconception floating around. Sometimes, when people talk about payroll tax, they're really referring to the combination of federal and state taxes in addition to the aforementioned social programs. However, it's important to note that income taxes and payroll taxes are two separate things. The confusion typically comes because both forms of tax are withheld from regular paychecks when the taxpayer is an employee. So remember payroll taxes as a distinct category separate from income taxes. These are an additional 15.3 percent tax on all pay.

If you're an employee, you typically pay half of the required payroll taxes, while your employer takes care of the other half—you pay 7.65 percent and your employer pays 7.65 percent to make the total of 15.3 percent. If a single earner makes more than $200,000, or a married couple makes more than $250,000, the total increases by 0.9 percent.

If you're a business owner, the rules change. You're responsible for the entire 15.3 percent of your wages. However, the word "wages" carries a different meaning depending on your business structure. After all, some self-employed people pay themselves the entirety of the business's profit as their wages, while others make investments in the business's name. So, for tax purposes, the IRS developed specific rules to define "wages" depending on the business's structure. This determines wages, thus determining the amount liable for the 15.3 percent tax rate.

Two Payroll Tax Structures

If you're a single-person LLC or sole proprietor, the IRS sees your income like this:

Revenue – Expenses = Owner Wages.

Now, most people would view that formula as the formula to determine profit. In essence, every dollar of profit in that setup is subject to the full 15.3 percent in payroll taxes. Again, that comes *in addition* to federal and state income taxes. This extra bit is often colloquially referred to as self-employment tax, though technically it's just the owner covering both halves of payroll tax. Still, for self-employed people, it certainly feels like they're paying an additional penalty just for running a one-person business.

For an S corporation, the formula changes somewhat. In this structure, the owner takes payroll separate from the rest of the company's profit. So, the formula looks like this:

Revenue – Expenses (including owner wages) = Profit

In this setup, the owner's compensation is part of the expenses. It is the only piece of the puzzle subject to payroll and income taxes. It's a difference in reporting. The income to the individual (the business owner) is reported as an expense to the business. The amount reported as profit is subject to income tax, but not payroll tax.

Do you see how this could benefit someone who wanted to save on payroll taxes?

In an LLC or sole proprietorship, you pay income taxes and an additional 15.3 percent payroll tax on wages, salaries, and tips that are paid to employees. In an S corp, you save that 15.3 percent from the profit, only paying it for your direct wages.

The Benefits of S Election

That's where S election comes in. It could be a strategy saving hundreds or thousands in taxes each year, depending on the firm's overall earnings and the owner's level of compensation. It requires incorporating as an S corp, or restructuring into one if you currently exist as an LLC or sole proprietor. This comes with specific requirements and benefits.

Besides reducing your payroll taxes, there are other benefits of having an S corp.

1. You get tax-free money up to the standard deduction as a benefit.
2. You can use the money coming into your S corp to make Roth contributions. (Annual Adjusted Gross Income limits apply.)
3. You can open a company-sponsored retirement plan that you can benefit from.
4. On top of this, you can bring your spouse and/or children in as employees and allow them to benefit from the retirement options.

To illustrate these benefits, imagine you had a spouse and two children on the payroll of your S corp. You can begin a company-sponsored retirement plan. Employees (not owners) in this situation can make salary deferral contributions to the retirement plan based on their compensation. The employer can also match contributions to the plan using the business's income. So you could take out the wages you need as the owner and pay the payroll taxes on it. Then, you can use the rest of the profit toward matching retirement contributions for your spouse and children.

Let's do some math. Each of your three employees can individually contribute $20,500 to their own 401(k) plan. That's the annual contribution limit at the time of this writing. However, the overall contribution limit to a 401(k) is currently $61,000, meaning the business itself can contribute $40,500. For all three employees (the spouse and two children) combined, that's $183,000 going into tax-deferred retirement accounts.[7]

The owner can also make elective contributions from their income up to the limit of $20,500 or nonelective contributions up to $61,000 or 25 percent of their income, whichever is smaller. Long story short, it can give you excellent retirement options on top of tax savings.

This doesn't necessarily mean everyone should try to become an S corp, though. There are administrative expenses, like processing payroll and filing an additional tax return. It also requires an additional level of documentation, and perhaps more scrutiny from the IRS.

This could give the strategy a significantly diminished return depending on the size of the business. It's not an automatic "yes" in every situa-

---

7   U.S. Department of the Treasury, Internal Revenue Service, "Retirement Topics - 401(K) and Profit-Sharing Plan Contribution Limits," IRS, accessed July 15, 2022, https://www.irs.gov/retirement-plans/plan-participant-employee/retirement-topics-401k-and-profit-sharing-plan-contribution-limits.

tion. But it is something to consider for every business owner wanting to save on payroll taxes.

Chapter Summary

On top of federal and state income taxes, payroll is subject to a 15.3 percent tax. For many businesses, this means employees pay 7.65 percent and the business itself pays the other 7.65 percent. However, for sole proprietors and single-employee LLCs, the owner is subject to payroll taxes on all of their profits, due to the way payroll taxes are calculated in this instance.

The rules are more favorable for S corporations, which must pay payroll taxes for the owner's compensation, but not for the other profits. These other profits can be reinvested, for example, into employer-sponsored retirement plans. This dovetails with the fact that S corps can hire the spouse and children of the owner, creating an opportunity to save on payroll taxes while contributing large amounts to tax-deferred retirement plans.

Chapter Takeaways:

✓ Check to determine whether electing to become an S corporation is right for you. It could be a good fit if you are a high-income earner whose business is currently structured as an LLC or sole proprietor.

✓ Becoming an S corp will save you a 15.3% tax on your profit, which is your income minus your expenses (including your own compensation).

✓ If you have a spouse and children, consider employing them and using some of the business's income to match or make nonelective contributions to the plan.

Strategy #20:

Using the Augusta Rule to Generate Truly Tax-Free Income

T ruly tax-free income of any kind is difficult to come by. All of your income and long-term capital gains are taxed unless you find a way to offset them. We discussed some of these strategies in Strategy #11. Still, you end up getting taxed *somewhere*.

The same goes for retirement savings. You can use tax-deferred retirement accounts to lower your taxable income on the front end, but you will get taxed when you choose to make distributions (or are required to make distributions) during retirement. If you go for the tax-free retirement route with, say, a Roth IRA, you are liable for income tax on your contributions the year you contribute.

Long story short, Uncle Sam always collects his due. The house always wins. Well, most of the time, anyway. There are a few ways to ensure that 0 percent of your income is subject to state or federal taxes, but almost none of them benefit you directly without risks.

First, there's the Qualified Charitable Distribution (QCD), which we talked about in Strategy #15. QCDs are distributions from your tax-deferred retirement plan that are sent directly to the charitable organization of your choice. So you get a tax deduction when you first invest the money, but you don't get to use any of the distributions. However, the money comes in and goes out completely tax-free.

Second, there are municipal bonds. We discussed them during Strategy #3, which was all about tax-aware investing. Municipal bonds are investments requested by city, state, or federal government to fund specific programs. Because you're funding the government, there are specific tax benefits for these bonds. These are good options for high-income earners who are maxing out traditional retirement channels, but they shouldn't be relied upon solely.

Third, you can harvest long-term capital gains at a tax rate of 0 percent if your Adjusted Gross Income (AGI) is low enough. For married couples filing jointly, the threshold is $83,350 as of 2022. This could happen toward the start of one's career when they naturally fall into the lower bracket, or if they have a lower AGI during retirement due to high investments into tax-exempt retirement plans. Furthermore, the taxpayer could use various methods to lower their AGI under the threshold if they're just above it, which we also covered during Strategy #11.

However, there is a fourth strategy, one that requires *zero investment* into the market, wherein the taxpayer can reap the full benefits of their income. It comes thanks to the Masters Golf Tournament.

The Augusta Rule

Yes, you read that correctly. The golf tournament, famous for its green jackets, led to one of the most beneficial tax rules for savvy taxpayers. The Augusta Rule is aptly named after Augusta, Georgia, the annual host of the Masters Golf Tournament.

As one of the most prestigious tournaments in professional golf, it draws thousands of fans and media to the course every year, not to mention the golfers and their teams. Because of this, many homeowners on the course rent their houses out to visitors during the tournament. For the rest of the year, they use their houses as normal. So, essentially, they become rental property owners for just one week. But before this, there weren't any provisions in the tax code for extremely short-term rentals. This was before the days of Airbnb and Vrbo.

To accommodate this, the Augusta Rule was created. The Augusta Rule allows homeowners to rent out their home tax-free for fourteen days or fewer each year. Now, this doesn't mean "the first fourteen days are tax-free." If you rent out your home for more than fourteen days, the rule no longer applies to you, and you have to pay taxes on the rental income. So, the rental period has to be fewer than fourteen days total. If you're curious about what qualifies as a "day," then check out IRS Topic 415.[8]

Now, the income still needs to be reported. It's the IRS we're talking about here, after all. To use the Augusta Rule, you need to complete Schedule E on Form 1040 and show the income you generated. Then, you need to offset the same amount of income on the "Other Deductions" line of the same form. Make sure that after the math is done, the amount of taxable income carried to the 1040 from your rental is $0.

You don't have to pay any taxes whatsoever on this income. Plus, since the amount reported is $0, this income doesn't even raise your AGI for tax bracket purposes. So you can combine this with other strategies, like harvesting enough capital gains to bring your AGI to the threshold (but not over). You can also combine it with business expense deductions, which we'll cover in a moment.

First, a caveat. No, you cannot rent your property out for an exorbitant amount and then get all that income tax-free. If that were the case, someone could theoretically filter all their business income through the rental property and go completely tax-free. The IRS won't have that. The rental income from your property has to be based on fair market rent, and you have to be able to prove it. How do you ascertain fair market

---

8   U.S. Department of the Treasury, Internal Revenue Service, "Topic No. 415 Renting Residential and Vacation Property," IRS, 2019, https://www.irs.gov/taxtopics/tc415.

rent? The simplest way is to hop onto one of the aforementioned apps like Airbnb and Vrbo and see what your neighbors charge for their properties.

And yes, you can rent your property to a business you own using this rule.

An Example from Real Life

So how could this work in a real-life situation? I'm glad you asked. There is a financial advisor in my network who uses his home for company meetings with his team. It could be an annual vision retreat or team-building event, but his business uses the home for two weeks out of the year.

He dutifully records the activities and minutes of this time, to demonstrate that the space was indeed used for business activities. This allows him to use the business to pay for the rental space and get a tax deduction for the expense. Then, he fills out his Schedule E along with his 1040 to report the rental income and deduct it entirely.

If he has fourteen meetings like this per year and charges $1,000 per day (according to the fair market rent of the property), he can create $14,000 in tax-free income each year. Plus, he can get a deduction for business expenses for his firm. Depending on his marginal tax rate, this could save him nearly $5,000 in federal income taxes every year.

The power behind this, like so many strategies, is the effect over time. We've discussed the law of compounding returns several times throughout this book because it really works. Five thousand dollars in tax savings is good, but over twenty years of applying this strategy, it turns into $100,000. If that money is dutifully invested in an account with compounding returns, it could become millions of dollars over the course of a lifetime.

Chapter Summary

The Augusta Rule allows you to generate truly tax-free income, which as we know from the rest of this book's content, is an extremely rare situation. Named after Augusta, Georgia, the home of the Masters Golf Tournament, it allows you to gain fourteen days of rental income tax-free.

It requires you to have no more than fourteen days of rental income for the year, and the income has to come at fair market rent. If you follow these requirements, you can rent your own home out to a business you own (like a business retreat). This creates personal income tax-free and gets written off as a business expense.

Chapter Takeaways:

✓ If you're a homeowner and own a business, you should rent your home to your business for two weeks each year.

✓ Set the rental expense at fair market rent and report the income (and the 100% deduction) using Schedule E.

✓ This will give you the rental income tax-free without raising your Adjusted Gross Income at all.

Conclusion and Invitation

Y ou made it!

Congratulations on making it to the end of this book, and thank you for investing the time and effort to get here. Our hope for you is that you can engage with taxes confidently for the rest of your life and ensure that your retirement and legacy are covered. Before our final encouragements, let's briefly summarize the content we've gone over to help you remember it as you go.

In the beginning, we covered the biggest myths we've encountered regarding taxes. The goal of this section was to help you determine whether you believed any of them and to familiarize you with the truth. We referred to this as the foundation of the rest of the book. After all, the twenty tax strategies we covered later wouldn't help a reader at all if they still believed something like Myth #3, which states "As long as I get a tax refund, I've won."

Then, we covered the basic building blocks when it comes to effective tax strategy. This included tax brackets, tax-deferred versus tax-exempt retirement plans, Required Minimum Distributions, state versus federal rules, and the importance of documentation. With the foundation set, we gained an understanding of the materials we'd use to build our overall tax strategy. Because of this, we consistently referred to the building blocks during the next section.

The third section included twenty strategies to ensure the taxpayer not only avoids getting killed on taxes but also develops a holistic strategy to building wealth and experiences the retirement of their dreams. This involved general strategies like tax-advantaged retirement accounts and investing with taxes in mind, all the way to specific tactics like Qualified Charitable Distributions or converting your business into an S corp.

We designed the contents of the book to enable readers to use it as a reference even after their first read. We hope that as you go into your next tax season, or find yourself with a sudden windfall, you can go back and brush up on the specific strategies you can employ to lower your tax obligations and make your money work for you.

To help you during your next tax season, we've created a free resource you can use as a reference. We call it the Tax Preparation Guide. When tax time rolls around, you can use it as a checklist to ensure you get all the deductions you're entitled to. Remember, the goal here isn't to get a huge refund, but rather to lower your tax liability from year to year or over your lifetime. To get it, just visit DontGetKilledOnTaxes.com.

Finally, we have additional resources and information online to help you take advantage of all the tax savings you're entitled to. Some of them go in-depth about practical ways to implement the strategies we've discussed so far. Others introduce more advanced strategies that build upon what you've already learned. To learn more about these, visit DontGetKilledOnTaxes.com.

Don't hesitate to reach out on that platform if you have any questions about implementing the strategies or using the building blocks. This is our final encouragement to you: Don't stop learning, and don't surrender the newfound control you have over your finances. You have the power to change your own life as well as your descendants' lives. Even when it feels intimidating, keep learning, keep documenting, and continue to look through the front windshield instead of the rearview mirror. Surround yourself with like-minded friends and advisers who can help you along the way … and enjoy the wealth you gain from not getting killed on taxes. After all, *it was your money all along.*

About the Authors

P. J. DiNuzzo

P. J. DiNuzzo is the Founder, President, Lead Consultant, Chief Investment Officer (CIO), Chief Compliance Officer (CCO), and Director of Business Development for DiNuzzo Private Wealth, Inc./DiNuzzo Middle-Market Family Office™/DiNuzzo Wealth Management, which has operated as an SEC Registered Investment Advisory Firm since 1989 and manages $929 million in Assets Under Management as of December 31, 2021. P. J. has devoted his entire professional career to indexing/efficient market theory, retirement planning, and educating the public regarding their benefits. He was approved as one of the first one hundred advisors in the United States with Index Research/Development Leader and Institutional Mutual Fund Manager, Dimensional Fund Advisors (DFA) in the early 1990s. DiNuzzo Private

Wealth, Inc./DiNuzzo Middle-Market Family Office/DiNuzzo Wealth Management was one of the first few hundred fee-only firms in the US in the late 1980s and has been consistently ranked as one of the top five hundred firms in the country by multiple national publications. Under P. J.'s leadership, DiNuzzo Private Wealth, Inc./DiNuzzo Family Office/ DiNuzzo Wealth Management, on numerous occasions, has been recognized as one of the "Best Places to Work" and was awarded the honor of "#1 Best Place to Work" in Western Pennsylvania/Pittsburgh in 2008, 2013, and 2016 by the *Pittsburgh Business Times*. Additionally, P. J. has been awarded the prestigious multiyear designation as a Five Star Wealth Manager. The award is given to Wealth Managers in Pittsburgh and across the US who satisfy key client criteria and score the highest in overall client satisfaction.

P. J. has earned the distinguished Personal Financial Specialist (PFS™) designation. The American Institute of Certified Public Accountants (AICPA), a national professional organization of CPA professionals grants the PFS credential only to certified public accountants with a significant personal financial planning education and experience. Candidates must meet six necessary requirements including an arduous technical exam and a peer review of their ability to demonstrate significant experience in a wide range of comprehensive personal financial planning disciplines.

P. J. has been interviewed on numerous occasions regarding Middle-Market Family Offices, Closely Held Businesses, High Net Worth Individuals, Strategic Asset Allocation, Portfolio Diversification, Indexing, Rebalancing, and Retirement Income Planning on various Television and Radio programs including *Private Wealth Magazine* with Russ Alan Prince, *Oprah & Friends* with Jean Chatzky on XM Radio, *Power Lunch* on CNBC, KDKA-TV2's *Sunday Business Page* with Jon Delano, *The Lange Money Hour* radio show with Jim Lange, ABC TV9 WCPO.com, and The Street.com TV.

P. J. has also been interviewed and quoted on a number of occasions regarding Strategic Asset Allocation, Portfolio Diversification, Indexing, Rebalancing, and Retirement Income Planning in various national, regional, and local magazines including *Kiplinger's Personal Finance* Retirement Planning, MarketWatch from Dow Jones, *Morningstar, SmartMoney, BusinessWeek, Investment Advisor, Financial Planning, NAPFA Advisor,* the *Wall Street Transcript, Wealth Management Exchange, Wealth Manager, Bottom Line Personal, InvestmentNews, Financial Advisor,* and IARFC's the *Register.*

He has also been interviewed and quoted on numerous occasions regarding Strategic Asset Allocation, Portfolio Diversification, Indexing, Rebalancing, and Retirement Income Planning in various national, regional, and local newspapers and websites including the *Wall Street Journal, Barron's,* Reuters, Bankrate.com, CBS News, YAHOO! Finance, *Pittsburgh Post-Gazette,* U.S. News & World Report, MSN Money, *Chicago Sun-Times,* FT.com *Financial Times,* SmartMoneySelect.com, the *Atlanta Journal-Constitution, St. Louis Post-Dispatch,* Chicago Board Options Exchange, *Pittsburgh Business Times,* the *Sharon Herald,* the *Christian Science Monitor,* the *Beaver County Times, Pittsburgh Tribune-Review,* MutualFundWire.com, *Gulf News,* TMC.net, Comcast.net Finance, Rydex Investments, FreeRealTime.com, Individual.com, Lockheed Federal Credit Union, Invest 'n' Retire, ABC TV9's WCPO.com, *Fort Worth Star-Telegram,* KYPost.com, Jim Prevor's *Perishable Pundit, Reading Eagle,* the *Toledo Blade,* Horsesmouth, DemocraticUnderground.com, the Community Investment Network, *Daily Herald,* Scripps News, the *Modesto Bee,* Hitched, Prime, *El Paso Times,* Paladin Advisor, Advisor Max, Denverpost.com, Oswego Daily News, The Dollar Stretcher, the *Ledger,* the *Columbus Dispatch, Savannah Morning News,* and Hampton Roads News Channel.

P. J. is a member of the Financial Planning Association (FPA), the Family Office Club, the Estate Planning Council (EPC) of Pittsburgh, the American Institute of Certified Public Accountants (AICPA), the Pennsylvania Institute of Certified Public Accountants (PICPA), the AICPA's National CPA Financial Planning Insights Panel, the National Association of Tax Professionals (NATP), the Financial Educators Network (FEN), and the Pittsburgh Society of Investment Professionals (PSIP).

P. J. chose football in lieu of a Major League Baseball offer from the Houston Astros to play with their Class A Team, as he attended and played football at Indiana University under Head Coach Lee Corso in the "Big Ten" (Bloomington, Indiana) and also at the University of Pittsburgh under Head Coach Jackie Sherrill. He later received his Bachelor of Science in Business Administration from Geneva College in Beaver Falls, PA. His graduate studies culminated in a Master of Business Administration (MBA) from the Katz Graduate School of Business at the University of Pittsburgh and a Master of Science in Tax Law (MSTx) from Robert Morris University at the downtown Pittsburgh campus. P. J. received his Certified Public Accountant (CPA) designation from the State of Delaware.

P. J. was a member of the Investment Committee on the Endowment Board for Valley Care Associates, a nonprofit organization providing adult day care, home safety consulting, and physical modifications for the elderly in Allegheny and Beaver Counties. He serves as a Finance Council Board Member for St. Blaise Church and is a member of the Department of Finance Advisory Board for Robert Morris University. He is a volunteer for and supports Habitat for Humanity and the Red Door Program for the homeless, and he is committed to his churches in Midland and Pittsburgh's South Side. He serves on the Board of Directors and volunteers for Hope House and The Center, both of which are located in Midland, PA, and support the women and youth of the community. He is a lifelong resident of the Pittsburgh and Western Pennsylvania area. He devoted over twelve years to helping and assisting numerous young men in Pittsburgh's inner city and surrounding areas by supporting and coaching over one thousand basketball games at the Amateur Athletic Union (AAU), elementary, middle school, junior high, and high school levels, attempting to teach and instill in them teamwork, trust, structure, discipline, and hard work.

Steven Jarvis

Steven Jarvis, cofounder, CEO and Head CPA of Retirement Tax Services, has never been a stereotypical accountant. Steven received his Bachelor's degree in accounting from Brigham Young University–Idaho and his Master of Business Administration from Eastern Washington University and is a licensed Certified Public Accountant (CPA). While he has put the years in behind a keyboard, he has always found other ways to engage and connect with people around him.

Steven was an adjunct professor at Whitworth University in Spokane, WA, from 2018 to 2020, cohosts a tax-focused podcast (the *Retirement Tax Podcast*) that thousands of taxpayers tune in each month, hosts a podcast teaching financial advisors how to deliver more value through tax planning, and is a nationally recognized speaker on tax-related topics. Steven also writes extensively, having been published in U.S. News, Advisor Perspectives, and Rethinking65, along with the regular articles he writes for Retirement Tax Services.

In addition to his work redefining what should be included in a tax preparation relationship, Steven is active with his family and always looking for an adventure. Along with his wife and two kids, Steven loves traveling, being outdoors, running races, and simply enjoying life. He embraces his inner "tax nerd" but thrives on all the fun things he gets to do with friends and family that have nothing to do with the tax code.

A free ebook edition is available with the purchase of this book.

To claim your free ebook edition:

1. Visit MorganJamesBOGO.com
2. Sign your name CLEARLY in the space
3. Complete the form and submit a photo of the entire copyright page
4. You or your friend can download the ebook to your preferred device

Morgan James **BOGO™**

A **FREE** ebook edition is available for you or a friend with the purchase of this print book.

CLEARLY SIGN YOUR NAME ABOVE

Instructions to claim your free ebook edition:
1. Visit MorganJamesBOGO.com
2. Sign your name CLEARLY in the space above
3. Complete the form and submit a photo of this entire page
4. You or your friend can download the ebook to your preferred device

Print & Digital Together Forever.

Snap a photo

Free ebook

Read anywhere